"As Jesus-followers, we always wan̲ᵗ ᵗ but communicating truth with grace can be challengin̲ᵍ ᵃᵗ times. Thankfully, *Real Love in an Angry World* offers wise instruction on how to practically guide people toward Jesus without pushing them away."

—Craig Groeschel, pastor, Life.Church;
author of *Divine Direction: 7 Decisions
That Will Change Your Life*

"How do we speak the truth in love? It's one of the trickiest and sorest subjects for Christians. Pastor Rick has gifted us a life-giving tool in *Real Love in an Angry World*, a guidebook to navigating those tough conversations. I would recommend this book to anyone who has beliefs and wants to voice them with charity and truth."

—Tommy Barnett, co-pastor, Dream City Church;
founder and co-pastor, Los Angeles Dream Center

"Pastor Rick Bezet doesn't shrink from relating the gospel truth concerning critical issues. He also uses amazing humor and true compassion to relate to each individual who hears that message. When Jesus spoke to the woman at the well, he began by relating to her need as a person before exposing the depths of her lifestyle. The book you are holding will help you do the same. The Jesus way. The compassion/truth way. The only way that will reach our confused nation and chaotic world."

—Larry Stockstill, pastor emeritus, Bethany Church

"One of many things I appreciate about *Real Love in an Angry World* is that my son knows the truth—not just facts, but truth that God loves us and is a lot more patient with us than we'll probably ever realize. Rick understands the importance of treating people with respect and honor, treating others the way he would want to be treated, even if he doesn't agree with them. He also knows how to live a fun life with joy and gusto. I love you, son, and I'm very proud of how you have become a real influencer of people."

—Richard Bezet Sr.

"I remember back when flip-flops became popular. Rick wore them all the time, but with white crew socks! As he proudly left the house every day, I would shout, 'Don't wear socks with flip-flops. You look like a geek!' But he ignored me and kept on. Before I knew it, he had all his friends wearing their flip-flops with white crew socks! That was the day I said to myself, 'This guy is a *leader*. Even when he looks like a geek, others follow him.' This was one of many examples from Rick's growing-up years that was evidence that he was destined to lead."

—JoAnn Bezet, also known as Mom and Ms. B.

"In an honest and hysterical way that only Rick Bezet can pull off, *Real Love in an Angry World* challenges its readers to live more like Christ and a little less like a Christian. It's a must-read for everyone wanting to cultivate richer relationships in their lives and learn just what it means to speak truth in love."

—Randy Bezet, lead pastor, Bayside Community Church

REAL
LOVE
IN AN ANGRY WORLD

REAL LOVE

IN AN ANGRY WORLD

HOW TO STICK TO YOUR CONVICTIONS
WITHOUT ALIENATING PEOPLE

RICK BEZET

BakerBooks

a division of Baker Publishing Group
Grand Rapids, Michigan

Published by Baker Books
a division of Baker Publishing Group
P.O. Box 6287, Grand Rapids, MI 49516-6287
www.bakerbooks.com

Printed in the United States of America

Library of Congress Cataloging-in-Publication Data is on file at the Library of Congress, Washington, DC.

ISBN 978-0-8010-1454-3

The names and insignificant details of the stories in this book have been changed to protect the identities of the people mentioned. Any resemblance of any person or situation, real or fictional, is entirely coincidental.

Rick Bezet is represented by Thomas J. Winters of Winters, King & Associates, Inc., Tulsa, Oklahoma.

17 18 19 20 21 22 23   7 6 5 4 3 2 1

Dedicated to
New Life Church,
for always looking for the next person
to welcome home.

Contents

Foreword

They are out there, but they are few and far between. People who bring joy to any and every situation; the ones who refuse to take life as it comes and instead redefine it based on their faith in God and daily choice to be a life-giving person. These individuals are so much more than the "life of the party" or "fun to be around" or a "peacemaker." Their words always seem to encourage you somehow, and their actions always speak louder than their words. These God-given friends make you reconsider your own life and how you're living it; they inspire you with their contagious attitude to be more grateful and more hopeful in every area of your life.

They are people like my friend Rick Bezet.

Rick is one of those guys with an irrepressible passion for life—someone I simply love being around. He is so genuinely positive that I always feel lighter after talking with him or hearing him speak. In fact, he brings light wherever he goes—both illuminating everything and everyone around him while also lessening the weight they often feel from life's burdens.

Rick also challenges me to see the truth of God's Word in dynamic new ways. He is truly a breath of fresh air. That's why I'm so thankful you're holding this book. Rick has taught me something we all need to learn and to live by: *life isn't what happens to you; it's how you respond to what happens to you.* This is especially true when it comes to your relationships and responding to people—not just your loved ones and other important people in your life, but everyone with whom you come in contact. As followers of Jesus, we're all called to be life-giving light-bearers, but unfortunately, we sometimes allow the cultural darkness around us to diminish our impact. We want to be positive, hopeful, and encouraging, but the negativism and critical spirit of our age feel overwhelming.

You don't have to go far to experience this friction. You see it in the news, observe it in politics, encounter it on blogs and social media sites, and face it in your community, workplace, and neighborhood. The culture around us has become so toxic, so opinionated, and in many cases, so downright mean that it has polluted our spirits and caused our hearts to be guarded.

Many people have resigned themselves to the fact that the only way to survive is to fight back. So we engage in the Facebook comment war, let the political battles ignite our rage, withdraw from people we once called friends, and at the very least, quietly form unhealthy opinions about others in our hearts. And before long, we too become toxic, defensive, resentful, bitter, and vengeful.

But this is not who God calls us to be, and it's definitely not the example we see in the life of Christ. As followers of Jesus, we are all called to respond a different way, a better way, and I believe that God wants to use Rick's experiences, story, and wisdom to help us live this life of love. More than ever, if we are to rise above the hatred simmering all around us, we need the life principles Rick teaches in this book.

I know that's a tall order. Few books deliver on their promise to improve your life. Too often, books contain a lot of hype and spin and too little relevant substance and practical application. Many authors know how to tell us what sounds good but fail to share what they've tested in the hard trenches of daily life. But that's not the case here. If you take Rick's message to heart, reflect on the truth of his teaching, laugh as hard as I know he will make you laugh, and apply the truths of God's Word, then I guarantee you'll learn how to be a person who brings light and life wherever you go.

You will know how to share *Real Love in an Angry World*.

Chris Hodges
Senior pastor, Church of the Highlands

1

Truth and Love

A couple of years ago, my dad was diagnosed with pancreatitis. He's healthy now, but for about a year, he was quite ill and I traveled to visit him as often as I could. During one visit, the doctors informed me that Dad wasn't going to live much longer. Maybe only a few hours. Dad is one of the funniest men I have ever known. You never know what he's going to say! But this was a serious moment.

"When you go in there today," the doctors told me, "you need to speak to him like this is the last time you'll ever see him."

My head was spinning when I entered the room. I was thinking about all the important things I wanted to tell him before I said my last good-bye. In that moment, I felt responsible to express my love and respect for him, to thank him for leading and loving me. So I did. I did it right! I honored my father in what I believed were the final moments of his life.

Then it was his turn.

Dad was alert but struggling to speak. I leaned forward. I hoped maybe he was going to say nice things about me, like I had just said about him, so I leaned even closer. Finally, he said, "I need to tell you something before you go." His voice was barely audible, a whisper.

"I'm listening, Dad. What do you need to say?"

"Tell everybody I died of AIDS."

I was shocked. "What are you talking about, Dad? You don't have AIDS. You have pancreatitis!"

"No. Tell everybody I died of AIDS."

I couldn't believe what he was saying. "Why?" I asked.

"Because I don't want anybody to marry my wife."

I laughed so hard. (See, I told you he was funny!) I couldn't live with *those* being his last words to me, so I asked, "Is there anything else you'd like to say to me?"

"Yeah," he said. "Come here. I want to tell you a true story."

"Yes, sir."

"This is true," he repeated.

"What, Dad?"

"Son. This is true."

I leaned forward, and he whispered, "Okay. A polar bear walked home from school one day—" I just totally lost it right there! Obviously this was *not* a true story. It took me forever to get my composure back so he could finish it.

"A polar bear walked home from school one day and asked, 'Ma, am I a true polar bear?' She said, 'Go ask your father.' The polar bear said, 'Dad, am I a true polar bear?' His dad said, 'Of course you are! Why do you ask?' He said, 'Because I'm freezing.'"

These are the two things my dad told me on his deathbed.

Then he said, "You have got to go. Leave." I walked out of the room. My dad didn't die, but I thought that was our last conversation. He missed a great chance to die right there.

My dad is not a liar. He likes to joke around, but he's an honest man who tells the truth. And he knows that in a dark situation, sometimes the truth isn't all you need. When you are navigating a dark and desperate situation, you may also need a heavy dose of love and joy. That's what this book is about. It's about helping you exercise real love in a world that desperately needs it.

Life-Taking Truth

My experience with church as a kid made me not want to have anything to do with God. As far as I knew, God was mad at me. I learned this from my legalistic church, which was more concerned about everybody acting the right way than actually reaching out to people.

I learned this truth from my Sunday school teacher, who seemed to enjoy torturing us.

She was the meanest person I've ever met. And she seemed to have it out for me. She would tell me, "Bezet, you are going to hell someday." I was eight years old! She talked about hell like she was born and raised there. She would ask, "Don't you want to go to heaven?" And I would say, "Not if you're going to be there, I don't."

One Sunday she was teaching on the Ten Commandments and mentioned never to take the Lord's name in vain. Without thinking, I blurted out, "Gaw-lee!" She stopped her lesson in midsentence, turned directly to me, and asked very slowly,

"What did you just say?" I answered with a quieter "golly" this time. She stared at me with her dark, stone-cold eyes, pointed at me with a knobby finger, and said, "Hell is hot, Bezet! Hell is hot! Hot! HOT!" Can you imagine anyone talking to a child that way and expecting them to discover the joy of the Lord?

I learned the truth that God didn't have time for me from one of our pastors at a church retreat. I'll call the pastor "Brother John," though that's not his name. He was one of the only people at that mean church who seemed kind. I can't tell you exactly why I felt that way. I don't remember him preaching about kindness. But something about him made me think he knew how to love someone.

That retreat took place during a season in my life when I really could have used some encouragement. My parents' marriage had been filled with arguments, disagreements, and more fighting and screaming than any kid should ever have to endure. Sometimes the tension felt as thick as a brick wall. For months at a time we didn't know where Dad was or what he was doing. Thank God my dad is serving the Lord now with all his heart. But that season was filled with a lot of uncertainty and stress. I was terrified of anyone finding out anything. I truly felt alone.

So I asked Brother John if I could go fishing with him. He said yes. I was so excited! I got up before daybreak the next morning, got my fishing pole, and met Brother John at the water. When I said hello, I could tell he wasn't happy to see me. We fished all morning, and he never said a word to me. If my line got snagged, he would sigh and roll his eyes. The longer we fished, the more nervous I got. Every now and then, I'd make a brief comment, but he wouldn't respond.

At the end of the day, I said, "Bye," but he didn't even acknowledge my presence. I thought something was wrong with me. And I continued to feel like there was something wrong with me—not just in Brother John's eyes, but in God's eyes as well. I just wasn't good enough to be around the pastor. To this day, I still struggle with the influence of growing up in that church. I often feel like I'm just not qualified to be in the ministry.

My truth, the truth I learned growing up in church, was that God was mad at me. That I wasn't good enough. That the only way to be accepted was to keep my problems to myself. That's not a truth that gives life.

The Good Part of the Past

Even though I hated church—and I thought the church hated me!—there were still many convictions I felt like I could depend on. Most people basically affirmed the sanctity of life. Most people basically affirmed the value of marriage and the family. But these days, it seems hard to find conviction. Anywhere. Two hundred years ago, Americans shared common values that were held in high esteem. We had our disagreements, but certain convictions, at least, were considered sacred. Take the Declaration of Independence, for example, which says, "We hold these truths to be *self-evident*." That means you don't have to explain them or defend them. They are clear and obvious to everyone.

Those days are gone. It happened gradually, and it has been happening for generations. But now it is clear that our nation has drifted away from the values we shared at the beginning.

Truth is no longer "self-evident." The change picked up speed starting around the 1960s. Since then, America has increasingly embraced the philosophy of relativism, the belief that different things are true or right for different people or at different times. It's where we get the phrase "You do you and I'll do me."

Because of these changes, many Christians today feel it is harder to stand for their convictions than it ever has been. They feel that fifty years ago everyone knew the answer to the question "What is truth?" But today our world of black and white has become a world of gray. That's an uncomfortable place to live. It would be easy to blame those outside the church for these changes. But the thing is, our secular culture isn't only to blame. We feel lost in a gray and angry world because Christians have failed to recognize and uphold the convictions that previous generations stood for. It's like Jesus said in Matthew 24:12, "Because of the increase of wickedness, the love of most will grow cold." Our world seems darker because our love has grown cold. This has happened in many ways. Here are a few.

Your Mama's Truth

One reason Christians have failed to resist the drift away from conviction and have lost sight of their first love is that many believers inherit their parents' beliefs and never make them their own. They pass from childhood into adulthood surrounded by their mama's truth, but they never embrace this truth for themselves. They never come right out and *deny* the Christian faith, yet they don't ever fully embrace it either.

But God doesn't have any grandchildren. At some point all people have to decide for themselves what they believe.

This is a problem especially in the Bible Belt, where I'm a pastor. People are exposed to the faith; it's available around them. But for too many who grow up in church, it never gets inside them. It's almost like being around faith has vaccinated them against the gospel.

The Israelites faced the same problem. God made it clear in the law that faithfulness is always one generation away from extinction. That's why after He gave the law to Moses, He commanded the people to keep the commandments on their hearts. The way to do this is to rehearse and repeat them. "Impress them on your children. Talk about them when you sit at home and when you walk along the road, when you lie down and when you get up" (Deut. 6:7). It's a great plan! But the Israelites failed. At the beginning of Judges, a depressing chapter in Israel's history, we read, "After that whole generation had been gathered to their ancestors, another generation grew up who knew neither the LORD nor what he had done for Israel" (Judg. 2:10). Why didn't they know the Lord or His deeds? Because their parents didn't teach the faith to them, and the children didn't make the faith their own.

I meet young people all the time who have no idea who God is and what He has done, even though they were raised in the church by Christian parents. They have access to the faith. They are in proximity to the faith. But it slips away from them.

Jesus knows we have a tendency to slip. That's why He prayed the way He did in John 17:15, when He said to His Father, "I'm not asking you to take them out of the world, but to keep them safe from the evil one" (NLT). "Make them

21

holy by your truth," Jesus continued. "Teach them your word, which is truth" (v. 17 NLT). The only way to embrace godly convictions is to cling to God's Word. The culture we're in would love to pull us far enough away from the Word that the cost of going back would seem like it's too much to pay.

Shallow Faith

Another way Christians have wavered from their convictions is that they settle for a shallow faith. Some of us take the first step and make the faith our own, but then we make a mistake: we learn one or two things and stop there. We dabble in the truth but fail to pursue it passionately. The result is that our knowledge isn't deep enough to support us when we face new challenges. We become like a football team that only knows one or two plays. Any sports fan knows that's a bad strategy.

Some Cajuns don't like Louisiana State University's football coach because he calls the same play over and over. Eventually, the opposing team catches on, no matter how dumb they are. I can say that because I'm an LSU fan. We Cajuns have cheers like this:

> Hot boudin, cold kush kush,
> Come on, team. Push, push, push!

And there's this one:

> Alligator, alligator, alligator, gar,
> We ain't as dumb as you think we is.

Some say it takes a Cajun two hours to watch *60 Minutes*, so that's how we cheer. But even a Cajun knows you can't run just one play. You can't keep your game simple, running the same old routes just because that's how you were coached growing up.

But that's what some of us do. We seemingly devoted Christians, whose love grows cold and who walk away from the faith, often do so because our faith was shallow to begin with. We hang on to one or two truths, but when those beliefs no longer work for us, we give them up completely. In fact, many of us are not confident about why we believe in Jesus or even *what* we believe *about* Jesus. For example, when a Muslim friend questions the Bible's teaching about Jesus and suggests that Jesus was a great prophet but not the Son of God, we don't know how to respond. Too often, when someone presses us about our faith, we come up with our own ideas without consulting the Word of God. Another way to say this is that when we aren't firm in our convictions, we tend to slip in with the culture around us.

We cannot change the truth. We cannot change God. He's not going to shift around with our latest ideas. A lot of Christians, though, instead of becoming more like Christ, ask Christ to be more like them. You can hear it in their dialogue: "Well, God didn't mean it *that* way," they say. "He said that two thousand years ago. If He was speaking in our culture today, He would understand." They mean to sound loving. But really they are compromising their convictions to make people more comfortable. This is not real love. This is evidence of shallow faith.

I have a friend who has a boat. (Everybody needs at least one friend with a boat!) He lets me take it out. I touch the buttons. It's awesome. But in one nearby lake, there are some dangerously shallow areas. You have to pay close attention when you're skiing there, because if you're cruising along at a high rate of speed and you hit a shallow area, the situation can quickly become dangerous. The way to stay out of the shallow water is to keep your eyes on the depth finder.

What is our depth finder in our relationship with the Lord, spiritually speaking? It's the Word of God. That's how we know how we're doing. When we're reading the Word, God will reveal to us when we're getting into shallow waters and our convictions are shifting. The Bible is our spiritual depth finder. Proverbs 5:1–2 says, "Turn your ear to my words of insight." Look at the depth finder. "That you may maintain discretion." Look at the depth finder. "And your lips may preserve knowledge," the knowledge of this Word. Look at the depth finder.

We're always moving either closer to or further away from the Lord. When you forget about the depth finder, when you start getting into shallow waters and your convictions start shifting, your heart and your decisions start shifting as well. If you're not paying attention, you may soon find yourself dabbling in things you never would have considered before. Look at the depth finder. Stay in the Word.

Just the Facts

Sometimes we fail in faith by losing our convictions—that's the mistake we've been talking about. But there's another mistake we can make, although it may sound strange to say it. It's also possible to fail by focusing only on our convictions and losing our love for God and others.

24

Some of us carefully study the Bible, formulate a theology, and develop a doctrine, but we never learn how to live the truth in love. When we make this mistake, we end up knowing a lot of information but not receiving much revelation in our hearts or transformation in our lives and relationships. Because nothing really changes on the inside, the way we relate to God becomes very black and white. That may seem like a good thing in an angry world. But it's really not. What happens is we turn our faith into a list of rules, and we determine the quality of our faith based on hard-nosed lists. The same thing happens to our relationships with others. If we make this mistake, we can become so judgmental, and so repulsive, that others don't even give God an opportunity to enter the equation of their lives.

This is a tendency I know well. I grew up in a very mean-spirited, legalistic church. The church I pastor now, New Life Church, throws a father-daughter ball every year. That never would have happened in the church I grew up in. No way! They thought dancing was evil. In fact, they denounced premarital sex because they thought it might lead to dancing. Okay, I'm joking. But just a little.

It's common for Christians to focus on defending *what* we believe, while neglecting to trust *Who* we believe in. Especially in a time when we feel judged or even persecuted for our convictions, some people are tempted to throw them away. Other people are tempted to double down on them. Yet we make a serious error when we reduce our faith to defending the "whats" of Christianity. There are ways we can relate the whats of our faith in the context of relationships. Truth isn't truth without love. The only way we will get this right is to first remember that truth has a name.

Truth Has a Name

John 18 opens in the garden of Gethsemane. Jesus has just spent the darkest hours of the night praying that God would find a way to cure humanity's sin problem without the cross. He has submitted to the Father's will, but it is a profound moment. "My Father! If it is possible, let this cup of suffering be taken away from me," Jesus prays. "Yet I want your will to be done, not mine" (Matt. 26:39 NLT).

Jesus was under so much pressure He started sweating blood. Then Judas brought some soldiers to the garden. He kissed Jesus's cheek to show which guy should be arrested, and the soldiers took Jesus into custody and led Him to the high priest to be questioned. Jesus stood before Pilate, a Roman governor. Here's what went down between them:

> Pilate then went back inside the palace, summoned Jesus and asked him, "Are you the king of the Jews?"
>
> "Is that your own idea," Jesus asked, "or did others talk to you about me?"
>
> "Am I a Jew?" Pilate replied. "Your own people and chief priests handed you over to me. What is it you have done?"
>
> Jesus said, "My kingdom is not of this world. If it were, my servants would fight to prevent my arrest by the Jewish leaders. But now my kingdom is from another place."
>
> "You are a king, then!" said Pilate.
>
> Jesus answered, "You say that I am a king. In fact, the reason I was born and came into the world is to testify to the truth. Everyone on the side of truth listens to me."
>
> "What is truth?" retorted Pilate. (John 18:33–38)

Pilate couldn't find a reason to punish Jesus. He probably thought Jesus was strange, but not criminal. But the point is, when Pilate asked the question, "What is truth?" he missed what was literally staring him in the face. The answer to Pilate's question is, putting it simply, that truth is not just a *what*. Truth is a *Who*. Jesus Himself is the truth.

One of the many unique things about Jesus is that He is the only sane person in history who claimed to be God. When others accused Him of talking and acting like God, He never denied it. Plenty of men have been deified by others postmortem, but not one of them staked claim to the title themselves. Muhammad did not. Buddha? Nope. Confucius? No, again. *Many* people through the years have said they were Jesus coming back to earth, but none of them volunteered to be crucified!

Here's the point: Jesus said, "I am the way and the truth and the life" (John 14:6). He claimed to be the truth! The apostle John explained this more beautifully than anyone:

> In the beginning the Word already existed.
> The Word was with God,
> and the Word was God.
> He existed in the beginning with God.
> God created everything through him,
> and nothing was created except through him.
> The Word gave life to everything that was created,
> and his life brought light to everyone.
> The light shines in the darkness,
> and the darkness can never extinguish it.
>   (John 1:1–5 NLT)

Unfortunately, just like today, the people of Jesus's day failed to recognize the truth when they saw it. Like Pilate, they missed the truth that was staring them right in the face.

The same thing happens today, even among people who call themselves Christians. People who abandon their convictions to fit in with their culture miss the truth when they wander from Jesus. Even people who stand firm for Christian convictions can miss the truth when their commitment to their convictions replaces their relationship with Jesus.

The Context Is Relationship

The bottom line is people struggle to stand for their convictions today because they think that truth is a *what*. They reduce faith in Jesus to holding the right ideas and adhering to the right concepts. When we recognize that truth is a Who (not just a what), our focus moves from *what* we know to *Who* we know. And that means we experience truth totally within the context of relationships. Our relationship with Jesus changes when we realize our ultimate goal is not to know *about* Him but to know *Him*, personally and intimately. Then, when we invite Jesus into our relationships with others, the truth transforms the way we relate to everyone around us. That's real love.

The laws of our land may change. Our understanding of right and wrong may change. But God's law doesn't change with the times. We, God's people, have to stick to our convictions. But if we view truth as territory to defend, instead of a relationship to share, our instinct will be to get defensive with others whom we consider a threat to our faith. Even the people who are "right" might not be right *enough* for our taste. If we have never made our faith our own or if our faith is shallow or if we have reduced faith to a list of doctrines and behaviors, we might view everyone as a threat at some point! When we get defensive about the truth, even the best-case scenario is pretty bad. We may (or may not) win an argument in the moment, but we will lose a relationship in the process. Paul knew this. Look at what he writes to a young pastor in 2 Timothy 2:24–26:

> And the Lord's servant must not be quarrelsome but must be kind to everyone, able to teach, not resentful. Opponents must be gently instructed, in the hope that God will grant them repentance leading them to a knowledge of the truth, and that they will come to their senses and escape from the trap of the devil, who has taken them captive to do his will.

Paul is talking about what it takes to bring real love to an angry world. Paul knew our testimony is only as good as our relationships. Never compromise, but lead with kindness.

Conclusion

Acts 22:15 says, "You will be his witness to all people of what you have seen and heard." To be a witness means to be *subpoenaed*. The word comes from the context of a courtroom, where if a person has the information needed to make a decision, they are brought in for questioning. They are subpoenaed. This is what the world is looking for when it interacts with Christians. Your neighbors are looking for a witness who will testify to them about real love. Your children are subpoenaing you, hoping you can show them real love in an angry world.

Real Love in an Angry World is designed to help you live as a compelling witness for Jesus in a world that desperately needs Him. My goal is for you to live in such a way that when you are subpoenaed by the world, the way you respond and the way you live your life in front of them transforms you, attracts them, and draws the world back to the light.

It may surprise you that this chapter has had so much to say about what Christians have done to miss the truth. I'm actually going to say more about that in the next chapter. Repentance is important in any relationship. We need to think about a few ways we've gone off track so that we can repent and move on in the light of Christ.

2

It's Getting Dark Out There!

My family and I were eating dinner at a restaurant when a woman I didn't know walked over to me and asked, "Are you Rick Bezet?"

I was reluctant to answer because she seemed angry. So I tried to stall by asking her a few questions. "What's your name? How are you this—"

"Do you pastor New Life Church?" she interrupted.

"Yes, ma'am. I'm *one* of the pastors—"

She interrupted me again. "I just want to know—right now!—if you believe in once saved, always saved."

"This is my family," I replied. "This is my wife, Michelle, my son Hunter, my daughter Hailee—"

She didn't care. She didn't care about my family. She didn't care about me. She didn't care if I was right with God or if I was experiencing personal revival. She didn't care if I had eaten my allotted amount of crawfish that season. She didn't care if my papaw had just died. She just wanted to know if I agreed with her issue.

We all have issues. If you don't think you have an issue, that's your issue! But we cannot become issues-driven people.

Conversations like the one I had with that woman happen to me all the time. "Which is better: large churches or small churches?" "Is there life after divorce?" "Do miracles still happen today?" "Is my dead cat in heaven?" (Your dog might be, but there's no chance for your cat!) "What's the right view of the end-times? Pre-tribulation, post-tribulation, or a-tribulation?" "And how do you baptize people? One denomination baptizes in Jesus's name only. Another says you must baptize in the name of the Father, Son, and Holy Spirit."

Several years ago, a young man in our church met Jesus and got saved. He was baptized at one of our services. It was a great day! Later, however, his mother was looking at the pictures from that day and realized that when he was baptized, his left ear didn't get totally submerged under water. She called us and went ballistic. She said, "My son is going to *hell* because *you* didn't baptize him all the way!" What I *wanted* to say back to her was, "No, ma'am. It's only his *ear* that's going to hell. The rest of him is fine!" (Think about it. Someone has to pastor this lady!) But I resisted.

Man, oh, man. I shake my head sometimes.

The conversations are not always about doctrine. Sometimes they're about morality or politics. "Should gays and lesbians be allowed to attend your church? Why wouldn't you host a rally for my candidate in your building?" Whatever the topic might be, what I sense when I'm around many Christians is that they just want to know—they *have* to know—that you agree with their issue, their platform in life.

I understand why they feel this way. Christians have been a majority population throughout the history of the United States until somewhat recently. Our Founding Fathers, many of whom were Christians, actually believed in a Creator. That's hard to miss when you read phrases like "endowed by their *Creator*" in the Declaration of Independence! You could easily argue that our culture has trusted the Ten Commandments as the basis for building a just and orderly nation. Even through rapid growth to becoming one of the most prosperous nations in history, the United States has honored Judeo-Christian values.

But over the past two generations, our culture has shifted significantly away from those core values. This is common knowledge, and many Christian writers have hashed this out in various books. I don't see the need to drive that point home again. What I *do* want to talk about is how Christians have responded to these changes. In my opinion, we have mostly responded in harmful and unhelpful ways. As our broader American culture has slowly but steadily abandoned traditional Judeo-Christian values, Christians have felt like they have to *do* something. That's true! We can't just stand around while America self-destructs. That's the right instinct. But we have responded to the culture drifting further away from traditional values by becoming more and more *issues*-driven.

It makes sense, if you think about it. It's easy to focus on the issues of the day. Social media is full of issues. The world is divided into camps and tribes, each one concerned about its issues and making sure everyone knows about them. Maybe we're not sure what else to do, what else to fix, so we cling to an issue. The problem is, when we throw ourselves into an issue—even when it's a good thing—we can completely lose sight of people. Jesus didn't say, "Go into all the world and address the issues." He said, "Go into all the world and make disciples."

Fixating on issues makes it hard to make disciples. When we focus on issues, we form teams that compete—it's *us* against *them*. We blame "the world," "those people" *outside* the church. We blame politicians, special interest groups with radical agendas, or secular humanists that forced the Bible out of our nation's classrooms. And then we start judging one another *inside* the church based on how well others support our issue. Now, all of those groups have contributed to the shift in values that we see in America today. But we won't make any progress until we realize "those people out there" aren't the only people to blame. We also need to hold another group responsible.

Ourselves. Christians. The church.

Yeah, the world is angry. The more Christians focus on issues, the angrier we become too. The world is getting angrier and the church is trying to keep up! But Jesus told His followers, "You are the light of the world" (Matt. 5:14). If the world is getting dark around us, it's because we as Christians have forgotten how to "let [our] light shine before others, that they may see [our] good deeds and glorify [our] Father in heaven" (v. 16). Who is making the failing grade here? Is it really the people who don't know Jesus? They are simply behaving like people who don't know Jesus! But many Christians out there are *also* behaving like people who don't know Jesus. That's on us.

Fruit vs. Root

In other words, by focusing on issues instead of people, the church has focused on the fruit, not the root, of the crisis. I believe we as the church have seriously failed America because we have failed to understand the *why* behind the *what*. Instead of worrying about whether someone is right with God, we want to know if they're on the right side of our issue.

When we get this way, we sound a lot like the religious leaders Jesus dealt with in the Gospels. One time the Sadducees tried to trap Jesus with a question about the resurrection. Here's what they asked:

> Teacher, Moses said, "If a man dies without children, his brother should marry the widow and have a child who will carry on the brother's name." Well, suppose there were seven brothers. The oldest one married and then died without children, so his brother married the widow. But the second brother also died, and the third brother married her. This continued with all seven of them. Last of all, the woman also died. So tell us, whose wife will she be in the resurrection? For all seven were married to her. (Matt. 22:24–28 NLT)

This is a weird question based on a weird law in the Old Testament, but I'm not going to get into that here. The important point of this passage actually comes just before this long question, in Matthew 22:23, which states, "That same day Jesus was approached by some Sadducees—religious leaders who say there is no resurrection from the dead." This verse tells us that the people asking this question, the Sadducees, didn't care if Jesus was the Messiah. They didn't care that

He had brought the kingdom of God. They just wanted to know where He stood on their issue. *Do You believe in the resurrection or not?* It's a funny question, if you think about it. Jesus not only believed in the resurrection, He *was* the resurrection (see John 11:25)!

Clearly, focusing on issues instead of people is a problem. Jesus dealt with it in His day, and it's a strategy He never recommended. In fact, Jesus didn't have any patience for religious people who got hung up on issues.

Another concern for religious people in Jesus's day was whether you shared your meals with the right kinds of people. Jesus ate with everyone, including people the religious types despised—tax collectors and prostitutes. The religious leaders couldn't stand it. They asked Jesus's disciples, "Why does your teacher eat with such scum?" (Matt. 9:11 NLT). Jesus overheard and answered them Himself. His response makes it clear He prioritized people over issues:

> When Jesus heard this, he said, "Healthy people don't need a doctor—sick people do." Then he added, "Now go and learn the meaning of this Scripture: 'I want you to show mercy, not offer sacrifices.' For I have come to call not those who think they are righteous, but those who know they are sinners." (vv. 12–13 NLT)

A Hundred-Year Walk of Shame

Most Christians today agree that the Pharisees missed the point most of the time. It doesn't seem fair to pick on them two thousand years later! So let's talk about a couple of examples from our own history.

One issue that a previous generation of Christians focused on was divorce. Christians have always valued marriage and the family, and people who didn't share that value were ostracized. Did you know that in 1890, three couples per thousand were divorced? *Three!* Per *thousand*! It's easy to see why there was a stigma associated with being a single parent in the twentieth century. Of course there was! But Christians handled it the wrong way. They distanced themselves from the mom who needed care and maybe some financial support, as well as from her kids, who needed mentors and a family that let them know they were okay. Some churches still do this. Some people don't want their own reputations to be ruined by the "mistakes" of a single mom's past (even if she wasn't the one who made the mistakes). They don't want *other* religious people to think they approve of her situation. So they keep their distance. She becomes one of *those* people out there. It embarrasses me when I hear about people who leave the church because Christians don't actually love their neighbor as they love themselves.

What the church *should* have done is extended grace through life-giving relationships to the women raising children without husbands. They should have reached out to the people, but instead they lashed out against an issue—divorce. This isn't just a history lesson for me. I lived it. My parents fought every Sunday on the way to church. When we pulled into the parking lot, my dad would adjust his collar and give my brother, Randy, and me a look that told us to put on a smile and keep our mouths shut. They knew they couldn't be honest with the people at church. They couldn't let anyone know they were having problems. If my parents had been in a church where they could walk in and be honest about what they were struggling with, maybe things would have turned out differently.

I hope this bothers you. You may be in a church that labels and judges divorcées. But that's not what divorcées and their families need—instead, the church should reach people like this!

Such ostracizing by the church still happens quite often. It's not uncommon for people to show up at New Life Church and say to me, "I was thinking about leading a small group, but I've got to tell you something. I got divorced when I was twenty-two." They may be only forty years old, but they feel like it's over for them. They feel like their past disqualifies them from leading today. There's no hope for them, other than just barely getting by—squeaking in.

Compared to those early twentieth-century stats, divorce today—which affects between 40 and 50 percent of all marriages—is so common we almost gloss over it. Maybe that's because we just don't know where to begin to reverse the trend. Perhaps we're faced with so many other stats that the divorce rate is just one more thing to be depressed about.

These days, since the divorce rate has risen so high, more and more unmarried couples are living together, not even raising the hope that a successful marriage is possible for them. Honestly, for a population that doesn't know Jesus, this strategy makes a lot of sense. It may *not* be possible, humanly speaking, for a man and a woman with no example of a successful marriage around them to make a commitment that lasts a lifetime. It's hard to be successful at something you've never seen anyone else succeed in. Because they don't know it's possible, they don't even try. Over time, we become a culture that devalues the marriage relationship. The responsibility for that process of devaluing doesn't fall only on the lost families out there or on the "gay agenda" or whatever. The responsibility also falls on Christians who won't reach out to their neighbors to help them restore their broken families.

A New Issue in Every Generation

The problem with the church is not the sin of the world. You heard that right! A lot of the problems with the world are because of the sin—the foolishness, even—of the church. Why is it that there is little variation between the divorce rate of the world and the divorce rate within the church? Because people, even Christian people, don't deal effectively with the truth. They think it's wrong for their marriage to fail, so when their marriage is failing, they hide out where the world hides out. They say, "If the church finds out we are this way, we are done." So they don't go to church. Or they go but keep their struggles to themselves.

I *wish* people would say, "Our marriage is in trouble. We need to get to the church! Someone there can help us." But that will never happen if we don't offer hope. We can't just say we're the hope of the world. We have to *act like* the hope of the world by actually offering real love.

One Sunday morning, a man came up to me in the church lobby before the service started. He walked straight to me, with his wife behind him, and their kids behind her. He said to me, "Hey, Rick. I'm probably gonna be kicked off the property for this—"

That's not a great way to start a conversation.

He went on, "My wife and I are not doing well. Last night it escalated. I didn't hit her, but I pushed her. Hard."

His wife and kids were staring at me.

"I just wanted to know if it was okay if I came to church today. I really need God."

This was a moment to push them away forever or draw them in, offer them hope.

I looked him in the eye and said, "You are exactly who we want at this church—people who have no chance without the hope and grace of God." Then I prayed with them. About two months later, the whole family got baptized. The couple went to counseling and saved their marriage. Their kids are now in college, serving God. Still, to this day, I look for them when I walk into church, and when they see me, his wife gives me a thumbs-up.

"Is it okay for *a man like me* to come to church?" Where does such a question come from? It comes from lots of experience being hurt by the church. It comes from years of the church failing to reach out to people in their mess. It comes from people in the church being just as angry and judgmental about someone else's issues as people outside the church.

Fog Lights

I grew up in Baton Rouge, Louisiana, where the humidity is off-the-charts high. People here in Arkansas will sometimes complain about the high humidity, but Cajuns just smirk. There are times in Louisiana when it is impossible to keep your windows from fogging up while you're driving. There is nothing you can do. You can wipe the condensation away and turn the defrost on high, but there is still more fog than is created by two teenagers parking! It can make driving extremely difficult.

More and more it feels like our culture is covered in fog. We don't know if we can drive around safely, because we can't see clearly. And if we make one wrong move, we end up in a ditch. Our nation has changed. Things we took for granted before, we can't just assume anymore. That's scary. But dividing over issues isn't the solution. It only ruins our witness in the world and makes us angry and destroys our love within the church. Division is not real love, and it will not change an angry world. The world must see our unity.

I'll admit sometimes unifying is difficult. For example, I once was told about a guy who started coming to New Life Church and seemingly fell in love with it. (Just so you know, I've changed this story a little, so the identity of this unfortunate fellow can be protected.) I had heard he was a church-hopper who took issue with every church he attended, but people began telling me he had put all his issues down. I started believing it, so I took him to dinner one night. Right in the middle of the meal, he put down his fork and said, "Let me ask you, Rick Bezet, do you believe in miracles?"

"Yeah, I do!" I said.

Let's just say, he still had an issue or two that was weighing him down. You would have thought I had told him I was the antichrist and Hitler was my sidekick. He went crazy on me. He called me a reprobate, or something along those lines. Then he left the church and starting telling people around town that New Life Church was full of false teachers. Friends, we're taking fire from both sides—from an angry world that increasingly rejects the gospel and biblical morality and from angry fellow believers who are so afraid of everything and everyone that they don't know what to do.

Why Are You Blaming Me for All This?

This is heavy stuff. But we've got to be honest with ourselves if we want to move forward. The church in America has dropped the ball repeatedly, which is why we're in the situation we're currently in. We want the world to walk in the truth. But that's not the world's job. It's the church's job to carry the truth wrapped in compassion.

So what's the answer? If focusing on issues isn't the way forward, what is? We have to walk the narrow road of truth and grace. That's how we will demonstrate real love in an angry world. Some Christians focus on "the truth" of an issue so closely that they miss grace altogether. That means we ultimately miss the truth too. Other Christians get the grace right but then water down the truth. Grace without truth isn't really grace.

I don't want to bring back ugly judgmentalism. I got enough of that when I was a child. And I certainly don't want to see Christians on the six o'clock news bombing Muslim neighborhoods or burning down abortion clinics. Can we have radical Christians? Absolutely. But there's just no room for radical Christians who are full of hate.

On the flip side, we can't be guilty of what I call "sloppy agape." Sloppy agape is generic love—love without wisdom, responsibility, correction, or conviction. Sloppy agape means we try to love someone by justifying their sin. A sinner walking away from a believer who loves with sloppy agape wouldn't know they're in sin or feel any need to repent of that sin if they just heard, "God loves you no matter what. Love wins!" How can that point people to Christ?

You hear sloppy agape when people try to assure others that "everything is okay" and "Jesus is all smiles" and "the world would be better if we all just cuddled up with Jesus." Not many people talk like that, but this is how they live. Sloppy agape is not real love. Jesus doesn't cuddle. He shoots straight with truth about your life, and then He backs it up with forgiveness—if you are willing to repent.

For example, He told the woman in adultery, "Neither do I condemn you. . . . Go now and leave your life of sin" (John 8:10). He then said to the crowd, "I am the light of the world. Whoever follows me will never walk in darkness, but will have the light of life" (v. 12). There is a condition in that statement: "whoever follows me." Jesus loves us, but the challenge to love Him back and live for Him is a consistent call. We must represent this balance of grace and truth. Real love is tough. Real love is pleading with sinners in an angry world, asking them with conviction to come out and find life.

Make no mistake, we simply cannot water down truth. Some may feel that a large church like New Life must be diluting the Word, but we strongly guard against that for two obvious reasons. Most important, we want to be a biblically sound church. Second, people are hungry for truth. I find people increasingly want to know straight up what the Word of God says.

The world doesn't dislike Christians because Christians are godly, honest, and stand for justice. The world dislikes us because we can be judgmental and without any wisdom or skill concerning relationships. That's because we've gotten real love wrong for too long. Let me ask you this: *Do people even want to be around you?* A lot of the resistance Christians now feel from the world, what we call "persecution," we've frankly brought on ourselves. Many of the tensions we feel when we try to live out our faith would disappear if we learned to navigate them with wisdom, grace, and common courtesy. When we do that, people will walk away from their encounter with us knowing we truly love them. Trust me, you can gain favor from others without compromising the Word of God. Jesus did it all the time.

Just to be clear, I'm not blaming the church for all the problems within our culture. But we do have to be willing to admit areas where we have failed. It's easy to blame "those people" out there for ruining America without ever taking responsibility for our own failures. The Pharisees in Jesus's day made the same mistake. They blamed the prostitutes and the tax collectors and the Romans and everyone around them for the predicament Israel was in. They blamed everyone but themselves. Jesus told them the issue began with them, in their hearts, not "out there" somewhere.

I'll go first. I'll admit there are times when I've contributed to this. There were times I pounded the table over an issue or two. I didn't like myself in those days, but I did it because I thought that was my calling. I thought it was the pastor's job to tell people what issues to care about and how to fight for them. But I don't like myself when I'm not a giver, and I don't like myself when I'm angry and judgmental. All I know is we can't be an issues-driven church if we want to demonstrate real love in an angry world.

We live in the finest hour in the history of the church right now. There has never been a time when the church could be more like Christ and win more people to the Lord. I have never seen people hungrier for the things of God than right now. The end-times may seem close by, particularly with rampant confusion, crazy political upheaval happening in many areas in the world, and Christians experiencing real persecution around the globe. But people are hungry for the things of God.

So how do we have a balance? Where we're not afraid of what's going on or of the future or of what the latest jihadist movement is up to? At the same time, how do we maintain a reverence for God? How do we hold to our convictions without being angry? In the following pages, I seek to resolve these challenges.

Where Is Real Hope?

Both Bill Clinton, the former US president, and Mike Huckabee, a two-time contender for the Republican presidential nomination, are from Hope, Arkansas. If you can say you're from Hope, then there are some great campaign slogans out there! But when we moved to Arkansas, I believed, as I do now, that the hope of the world is not government, legislation, or the past, present, or future president. I believe the hope of the world is in what the church has to offer.

When I read the Word, it's the same now as it was when I gave my heart to the Lord. I've said this for years—truth simply misses the mark if there is no compassion. When we as a church can rediscover the heart and the voice of Jesus and find that balance in situation after situation, while facing issue after issue, we can win our culture back to Christ.

Our hope, our *only* hope, is the gospel of Christ. That means our mission is the Great Commission. Jesus is the *only* name by which people are saved, so no other "issue" takes priority over sharing the gospel. We still have a major role to play in the Great Commission; God isn't finished using His church yet. You know how I know that? We're still here!

We have to learn how to share this message in an angry world. Romans 10:14 says this:

> But how can they call on him to save them unless they believe in him? And how can they believe in him if they have never heard about him? And how can they hear about him unless someone tells them? (NLT)

My friend, "telling them" is not just posting something on social media! It's not just yelling the truth across the room. It's not holding a sign at a rally or protest. Jesus got involved in people's messes. He walked slowly among the crowd. He gave sinners His time. He answered their questions. He prayed for them. You can't do that if you're intimidated by others who are different from you or if you're always fighting over issues. Instead, when you're moving slowly through the crowd, noticing people, the Spirit of God will lead you to help someone, to pray for someone, to make a phone call, to drop by and visit a hospital room, to write a note, to send a gift card, to be available in difficult and even intimidating circumstances. And by the end of this book, my hope is that you will be challenged to grow in confident compassion for the lost—that you will show them real love by fighting for their souls.

Our goal is spelled out in Ephesians 4. We don't fear the world outside the church. We don't fight and divide over issues. "Instead, speaking the truth in love, we will grow to become in every respect the mature body of him who is the head, that is, Christ" (Eph. 4:15).

This verse contains many challenges—and plenty of opportunities to mess up, frankly. What does it even mean, practically speaking, to speak "the truth in love"? How in the world do we become a mature body, like Christ "in every respect"? I hope you join a campaign with me to get every Christian to live in the center of the path where Jesus lives. Jesus is never moved into compromise (the ditch on one side of the path), and He is never moved into condemning others (the ditch on the other side). He is real love.

My hope is less about taking the culture back to Jesus, though I desperately would love for that to happen. My hope is to take the *church* back to Jesus. In so doing, we will represent Him more fully and accurately to a culture that desperately needs to know that God is not mad at them. And then, collectively, we will be able to bring Jesus to the culture.

Conclusion

I turn to Romans 12 often to clarify my vision and reorient my priorities. In verses 9–21, Paul spells out how to show real love in an angry world. He should know. The world he lived in was every bit as dark as ours. Here's how he describes our mission:

> Love must be sincere. Hate what is evil; cling to what is good. Be devoted to one another in love. Honor one another above yourselves. Never be lacking in zeal, but keep your spiritual fervor, serving the Lord. Be joyful in hope, patient

in affliction, faithful in prayer. Share with the Lord's people who are in need. Practice hospitality.

Bless those who persecute you; bless and do not curse. Rejoice with those who rejoice; mourn with those who mourn. Live in harmony with one another. Do not be proud, but be willing to associate with people of low position. Do not be conceited.

Do not repay anyone evil for evil. Be careful to do what is right in the eyes of everyone. If it is possible, as far as it depends on you, live at peace with everyone. Do not take revenge, my dear friends, but leave room for God's wrath, for it is written: "It is mine to avenge; I will repay," says the Lord. On the contrary:

"If your enemy is hungry, feed him;
if he is thirsty, give him something to drink.
In doing this, you will heap burning coals on his head."
Do not be overcome by evil, but overcome evil with good.

That passage is a lot to unpack. And it's easy to misunderstand. Some people read "Hate what is evil" and think it means "Hate evil people." It doesn't! For now, notice how much of Paul's instruction has to do with how to manage relationships. If I'm reading Paul right, it looks like the truth plays itself out in relationships. It's not about issues. It's about people. Relationship is where love happens. It's also where love falls apart. In the second half of this book, we're going to take a close look at how to show real love in our relationships—with those closest to us and those we might even consider our enemies.

But before we do that, we need to get firmly grounded in the truth. The only way to avoid sloppy agape is to make sure our love is rooted in God's Word, not in our feelings. So we're going to talk about the Bible. The Bible, the Word of God, shows us exactly what real love looks like in an angry world. That may surprise you if you think *God* is the One who's angry. He's not. And the Bible isn't a book of rules and regulations. God is *for* you, and He wants a relationship with you. And His Word is all about relationships. Our ability to love, for real, in an angry world begins with the most important relationship—our relationship with Jesus. If you want to know more about that, then turn the page.

3

Big, Ugly Bible

One of the many things I hated about going to church when I was a kid was that the pastor used King James English whenever he prayed. He used normal, everyday words when he preached or shook people's hands in the foyer. But he turned into Shakespeare when he prayed: "Our Father, we humbly thank Thee for Thy many blessings and for Thine everlasting and divine goodness toward us, Thy lowly servants." And on and on. When he finally said, "Amen," he'd use normal English again. I had no idea what he was saying when he prayed.

The reason he prayed that way is because we read the King James Version of the Bible in those days, and that's how *it* sounded. The King James Bible, which was translated in 1611, uses all kinds of words we don't use anymore. In Matthew 3:8, Jesus commands, "Bring forth therefore fruits meet for repentance." What? In other places, the King James

Version uses words we use today, but they mean something completely different now. So when James 2:3 says, "And ye have respect to him that weareth the gay clothing," it means one should not show special attention to the man wearing fine clothes. That's not what *I* would have heard as a kid. I didn't understand a word the pastor said when he prayed, and I didn't understand a word the Bible said when I read it.

Even though I didn't understand a word of the Bible, I was expected to read it. Every day. Early in the morning. I didn't want to read, and I definitely didn't want to read it when I would rather have been sleeping! How was I supposed to make sense of Proverbs 2:12—"To deliver thee . . . from the man that speaketh froward things"—before school? But my pastor and my Sunday school teacher made it clear that God would be mad at me if I didn't have "quiet time."

Maybe you can relate to this. Or maybe you can't. Maybe you've never seen or held or opened a Bible. Maybe this is the first "Christian" book you've ever read, and the idea of reading the *actual* Bible intimidates you. I can understand that too. The Bible is a big, old book.

Whatever your background is, learning to demonstrate real love in an angry world begins with the Bible. Many Christians can't experience real love because they think God is angry with them. They have to get rid of that idea. He's not! The only way to discard that idea is to get to know Him intimately and deeply. The place we meet Him is the Bible—this big, old book that we sometimes don't understand.

When I was a kid, I saw the Bible as two old books in one—the big Old Testament with a lot of words I couldn't pronounce and the little New Testament with fewer words

I couldn't pronounce. The Old Testament appeared to be a history book for the Israelites, with a ridiculously long set of complex rules. I thought God was constantly angry with those people who just couldn't get their act together. By comparison, the New Testament was easier to understand. It told a great story about Jesus, who healed both good and bad people and irritated all the religious people, then died and came back to life to meet with eleven leftover disciples. After that was a bunch of little books that talked about how we're supposed to behave. It all ended with a story of how the world is going to end in a terrifying ball of fire.

That's what I remember, anyway. But I didn't get all that from reading the big, old book. I got that from the pastor who sounded like the King James Version of the Bible.

Now that I'm a pastor myself, I know people are always going to be intimidated by the Bible until they realize what it's for and what it's about. Here's what I know. Through the years, I have come to understand that the Bible is not humankind's book about God; the Bible is God's book about Himself. It's an autobiography. God's autobiography. That means our main goal when we read the Bible is not ultimately just to know the Bible. Our goal is to know God, who reveals Himself in His Word. Many people have the same view of God that they have of the Bible. To many people, God is big. He's old. He's something to pull off the shelf once a year, maybe at Christmastime, but He's impossible to understand. The God revealed in the Bible is not all those terrible things people sometimes believe about Him. He is a God who wants to know you and wants you to know Him. He wants what's best for you. He wants to make the truth crystal clear.

That's where the Word comes in. His Word is a gift. He wants you to open it.

The Essence of the Bible

Second Timothy 3:16 says, "*All* Scripture is inspired by God and profitable for teaching, for reproof, for correction, for training in righteousness" (NASB, emphasis added). That's great. But "*all* Scripture" is a lot! We can't know "all Scripture" overnight. Many Christians have never read "all Scripture." So how can we know what the Bible is all about before we've read all of it?

Jesus answers this question for us clearly in the book of Matthew. Someone asked Jesus one day, "Which is the greatest commandment in the Law?" It was a tough question. There were 613 commandments to choose from. What this person wanted to know was, if you could take all 613 commandments from the Scriptures and summarize them in one sentence, how would you do it?

Here's how Jesus answered: "'Love the Lord your God with all your heart and with all your soul and with all your mind.' This is the first and greatest commandment. And the second is like it: 'Love your neighbor as yourself.' All the Law and the Prophets hang on these two commandments" (Matt. 22:37–40).

With one simple response, Jesus reduced 613 commandments down to two. He didn't delete any of them. He didn't say any of them were unimportant. Instead, He brought to the moment a synopsis of the entire Bible in two main points: love God and love people. These are the two most essential truths of all. If you do this, Jesus was saying, if you *really* do this, you will fulfill all 613 Old Testament commandments, even if you don't know what they are.

Jesus summarized the heart of the Bible in terms of relationships. The purpose of the Bible is to teach God's people how to love God well and how to love one another well.

When our kids were little, my wife, Michelle, and I didn't want to tell them they had to behave a certain way just because they were the pastor's kids. I didn't want them to hate the church or resent our call as a family to be in ministry. Instead, we told them, "In the Bezet family, we love people. In the Bezet family, we admit when we're wrong. In the Bezet family, we respect people." That's basically what God does in the Bible. He says, "In this family, we love each other this way. In this family, we forgive people. In this family, we love our neighbors as ourselves."

God knew that if He left it up to us to decide how to love Him and one another, we would get it all wrong. It wasn't supposed to be that way. God created Adam and Eve to fellowship with Him and to love and protect one another. But that all changed when the first humans decided they knew better than God how they should live. When Adam and Eve sinned in Genesis 3, they immediately felt distant from God and suspicious of each other. The closeness they enjoyed before was gone—just like that. We've been trying to get it back ever since.

Fortunately, because God loved Adam and Eve, He immediately started working in the world to restore His relationship with His people. He also began repairing people's relationships with one another. He did that by giving a gift— the law. Commandments. Now, the law doesn't always *feel* like a gift. But it's for our good. It's there, ultimately, to teach us how to love God and other people the way God designed us to love. That's the first thing we need to know about the Bible: it is all about relationships.

But It Was *So Great* Back There!

When we love God and love others well, we are living wisely. The thing is, we cannot carry on in the angry world that we live in with the same portion of wisdom we had last year. We don't learn everything we need to know all at once and then we're done. We have to encounter the truth regularly. A ten-year-old has only ten years' worth of life to give Jesus. A fifteen-year-old has a lot more to give God. We always have more to give away to the Lord the next year. We can't go on the wisdom of last year.

The children of Israel were once rescued from Egypt (see Exod. 12). They escaped slavery, but they still weren't totally free. They were delivered from the enemy, but not into the promises of God. The Lord guided them through the sea and the mountains, through the valley and the desert. It was a trip that could have taken just ten days. But God had them wander around in that dry place for a solid year as He took what must have seemed like His dear, sweet time moving them from Egypt to the promised land. The point of this journey was to give Israel time to receive the law, discover how to worship and love one another, and learn to trust God's provision. This example highlights one of God's many character traits—sometimes He takes a long time to get us where He wants us. He's patient with us, but we're usually not patient with Him.

God wanted the people to enter the promised land at the end of that year. But because the Israelites wouldn't listen to Him, they ended up going around and around in the desert for forty stinking years. That's the bad news. The good news is, every day they received manna from heaven to eat and water from a rock to drink. God made sure His people had every provision they needed.

The Lord told Moses, "I will rain down bread from heaven for you. The people are to go out each day and gather enough for that day" (Exod. 16:4).

The daily manna was their quota. Enough for that day. That was it. You see how it's all related? I want the church I pastor to be healthy, but I can't feed the congregation the Word of God with just one sermon a week. Even if I serve up a seven-course meal every Sunday—and I don't—that's still only enough for one day. On Monday, you have to feed yourself. You can't survive physically on one meal a week, and you can't survive spiritually on one reading of God's Word a week. You need God's Word every day. Jesus even taught us to pray, "Give us today our daily bread" (Matt. 6:11). He was talking about physical provision, yes, but He was also referring to spiritual nourishment.

I want to challenge you right now—whatever season you're in, however old you are—to make a commitment to get in the Word every day. God gives us from the Bible what we need for that day. But we have to be willing to receive what He has for us. We must give Him some time and read His Scriptures every day, even if it's only a few minutes.

Christians who aren't in the Word of God every day become emotionally driven, led by their feelings. They become like a person on a sailboat. Wherever the wind blows, that's where they're headed. A person who is led by faith, who stays in the Word, is like a person on a steamboat. Wherever the captain says we're going, that's where we're going.

A person can live for forty days without food. But a Christian shouldn't go more than a day without feasting on the Word of God. Before He started His ministry, Jesus fasted in the desert for forty days. No food. Satan approached Jesus and tried to tempt Him, saying, "If you are the Son of God, tell these stones to become bread" (Matt. 4:3). Jesus answered with what we should say when we're tempted: "Man shall not live on bread alone, but on every word that comes from the mouth of God" (v. 4). He was quoting the Old Testament (see Deut. 8:3) and giving us an example of how to use the Bible to resist the evil one.

Let's turn to real life for a quick illustration. A certain football team was facing the hottest game ever in its history. Temperatures were also predicted to be extremely hot on game day. So about a week before the big game, the head coach called the team together and basically commanded them to get hydrated every day throughout the week. Every day, every day, every day. He explained to them that if they waited until game day and then chugged a bunch of water right when they felt thirsty, they would simply have stomachs filled with water.

"We don't want that," he said. "We want it to be cellular—every cell in our bodies should be fully hydrated."

When game day arrived, the whole team had done what the coach had commanded. At the start of the game, the teams matched each other stride for stride. During the second half, however, the other team started cramping up and having major problems. The winning team—with the players who had stayed hydrated throughout the week—was able to pull out a major victory in the home stretch. All because they were nourished. They were hydrated.

I love the following scene from John 6:33–35:

> "For the bread of God is the bread that comes down from heaven and gives life to the world."
>   "Sir," they said, "always give us this bread."
>   Then Jesus declared, "I am the bread of life. Whoever comes to me will never go hungry and whoever believes in me will never be thirsty."

Recently I noticed that when I go on vacation, I don't read the Word every day. I get out of the routine and just don't stay in the Word. Then, even if I've been away for a week relaxing at a lake, I come back exhausted. I come home without energy when I haven't been in the Word. We need a daily helping of God's Word because we find Jesus in it. It's where He meets us. It's where He feeds us and hydrates us. It's where He changes us.

Show Me Something I Haven't Seen

The next thing you need to know about the Bible is that God wants you to find revelation in His Word. It is possible to read the Bible every day and never encounter Jesus there. It's possible to eat the daily bread and still live a weak and powerless Christian life. The written Word is essential, but it doesn't become powerful until the Holy Spirit plants it in your heart, until He has revealed the truth to you.

Sometimes the Word revealed to us gives us the "why" behind the "what." Sometimes it's obvious, like what we find in Proverbs 5:8–10:

> Keep to a path far from [the adulterous woman],
>   do not go near the door of her house,

lest you lose your honor to others
and your dignity to one who is cruel,
lest strangers feast on your wealth
and your toil enrich the house of another.

Over and over, Scripture warns us: "Don't do *this*, or *that* will happen."

Other times, the Word of God gently reveals something that prompts us to respond to God with a confession: "I've been doing this wrong. Can you help me with this?" In moments like this, God is revealing something *about* you *to* you that you haven't noticed before, or maybe you just didn't really want to see. However, *God* already knew it was there. It's possible everyone else around you knew it too! But it becomes a revealed truth to you when *you* notice it. It could be a simple new insight or a deeper understanding *for you*.

For example, Romans 3:23 says, "For all have sinned and fallen short of the glory of God." It's a simple verse many people are familiar with, and maybe you've even used it before as a blanket statement to demonstrate that everybody needs a Savior. And that's certainly true! But then at the end of a long day, maybe you're trying hard to finish a project when "that" person in the office gets on your last nerve and you say something stupid. Perhaps it isn't obvious to those around you, but you know you've blown it. You thought you had finally become a levelheaded person, but now you feel like you've got a long way to go.

Then you hear Romans 3:23 in your head, only it sounds more like this: "For *all* have fallen short." You realize in the moment that you're human, not superhuman, that God understands you, and that the blood of Christ covers *all* your sin. The first five hundred times you heard the verse, you understood the words in your mind but thought it only applied when you got saved. You have always agreed with the truth of this verse, but when faced with your own guilt—great or small—it brings a new level of humility in your heart. So you respond with something like, "Yeah, I messed up. I'm sorry, God." And then you are able to sincerely apologize to the guy you slammed five minutes before, because you know that it will bring you that much closer to God. That's revelation.

Sometimes I'll read a verse that at first means very little to me. But if I pray over it for a few days, thinking deeply about it, I eventually see that verse totally differently. That's revelation. When I come to a verse that seems intriguing, but I just don't understand it, I follow this meditation process.

Here's another example. Galatians 5:22–23 says, "But the Holy Spirit produces this kind of fruit in our lives: love, joy, peace, patience, kindness, goodness, faithfulness, gentleness, and self-control" (NLT). Maybe you've read these verses in the past in a way that made you feel defeated and left you wondering, *Will I ever be able to be kind to others?* Then the Holy Spirit whispers, "This is about the fruit of the Spirit, not the fruit of you! As you submit this to Me, allow My presence to be kind to others through you." And it dawns on you that the fruit of kindness is not dependent on your ability to will yourself to be kind to others. No, it's a submission issue. Submit to the presence of God in your life, and His presence will give you the power to be what you can't be in your own strength.

God has given us His written Word to consume. It is a gift we have to open. The written Word becomes the revealed Word when we "meditate on it day and night" (Josh. 1:8; see

Ps. 1:2). To meditate on something means basically to get deep into it, to mull it over or chew on it for a while. While you are thinking about what a passage means, it is a great opportunity to be in conversation with God about that passage. When you pray, *God, show me what I might be missing while I read this passage*, you are humbly approaching our gentle and patient Father, asking Him to show you things. He will gladly do it.

Jesus promised in John 16:13 to actively communicate with us through Scripture:

> But when he, the Spirit of truth, comes, he will guide you into all the truth. He will not speak on his own; he will speak only what he hears, and he will tell you what is yet to come.

The apostle Paul prays a similar thing in Ephesians 1:17:

> I keep asking that the God of our Lord Jesus Christ, the glorious Father, may give you the Spirit of wisdom and revelation, so that you may know him better.

Whether it's a passage you have been familiar with for a long time or a verse you just stumbled on yesterday, you can receive a revelation from the Lord that will change your life forever. Then, when you go back to that passage in the future, you will no longer view it the way you did before. More important, you will remember how that revelation has changed you.

Pray for it. Pray for the Spirit of wisdom and revelation. Ask God to guide you through His Holy Spirit. Ask Him to speak to you through His Word and to open your eyes as you go through your day. If you pray this consistently, you can expect to grow in discernment.

The first revelation I ever experienced regarding Scripture was Psalm 37:4, which reads, "Delight yourself in the LORD, and he will give you the desires of your heart" (ESV). Some people will tell you that the verse means if you delight in God, He'll give you whatever you desire. I was in line with that thinking until God helped me see it in a new way. It means that if you delight in God, then He *places* desires inside of you.

God did this for me. I grew up in Louisiana and loved it there. "I'll never move to Arkansas!" I said. Then one day I had a revelation from Acts 17:26, which states, "From one man he created all the nations throughout the whole earth. He decided beforehand when they should rise and fall, and he determined their boundaries" (NLT). I had read that verse before. But suddenly God revealed to me that He picks the places and the times we live in—including mine! In that particular revelation, I received from the Lord a desire to move to Arkansas. It came from a supernatural revelation, and now I can't stand *not* being in Arkansas. Simply put, I moved to Arkansas because God planted a desire for Arkansas in my heart. My love for eating crawfish—that's from God. But if you like USC football, clearly you didn't get that desire from God! No way! Okay, I'm kidding about that.

Or sometimes you get a revelation when you read a verse from a different perspective. Take, for instance, Proverbs 15:1, which says, "A gentle answer turns away wrath." You can initially read it like a nice saying that should hang on your kitchen wall somewhere. But then you read it like, "Hey, try responding to your wife a little differently when she tells you that you missed taking the trash to the street for the third week in a row." And the Lord begins to show you that you have a part to play, and your part then becomes letting the truth in the Word change you.

That's what a revelation is. It's so real and so alive that you can't believe you didn't know it before. It changes the way you live from that point forward. This is what God wants for you. He wants the Word to come to life in you.

You Can't Fix You . . . and Neither Can I

So why does reading the Word matter? What difference does it make? The answer, in a nutshell, is that the more you read it, the more God shows you things.

The more of the Word that is in you, the more you know the Word; the more you know the Word, the more you understand the character of the Author of that Word—Jesus. So the Word of God in you, plus the living, breathing presence of God in you, equals the power to overcome everything the world is throwing at you.

But get ready! Jesus always steps up the law. The Old Testament said, "Don't commit adultery," then Jesus came along and basically said, "The way you looked at her? You committed adultery in your heart." When I was a youth pastor, I would teach the kids that if they saw something tempting, to simply not give it a second look. Sometimes you have no control over what passes in front of you. But you do have control over the next look you take. One bold young man then asked me, "What if I look and never look away?"

Jesus always addresses heart issues. The cool thing that happened after the resurrection and ascension is that Jesus then sent the Holy Spirit to help us. He knew we couldn't succeed all on our own. He gave us His Word. And then He gave us His presence so we could succeed in obeying in His strength rather than our own. This is an essential truth: Jesus is the Truth, He is God's Son, He loves you, and He made a way for you to live a great life on both sides of eternity.

In all that, we discover that a relationship with Jesus is the ultimate fulfillment of the unilateral covenant God has made with humankind. That relationship grows as we spend time daily in the Word and in conversation with Him through prayer. Listen to me. I want you to hear this: God is not mad at you. He loves you and wants to be with you.

If you don't know Jesus as your Lord and Savior, if you don't trust Him with your life, then He doesn't have your permission to be in a life-giving relationship with you and you can't be around Him. It's really that simple. It's not that God can't stand to be in *our* presence because we're messed-up people. (If that were the case, Jesus wouldn't have been able to be around anybody. Think about it!) It's that *we* can't live in *His* presence with sin.

The Bible Is a Great Read

All this talk about reading the Bible may intimidate you. You may think, *Okay. I get it. The Bible is important. But it's also really big. Where do I start? How do I do this?*

First, find a translation you can understand. If you're brand-new to the Bible, I recommend you start out by reading a psalm (from the book of Psalms) and a proverb (from the book of Proverbs) in the morning, then a chapter in either the Gospel of Mark or the Gospel of John later in the day (check your Bible's table of contents and look for these books). If you're married, I recommend you read with your spouse for about five minutes, then spend about five minutes discussing what you read. If you aren't married, consider asking a friend to read the same passages you're reading and discuss them daily or once a week. It's also important to get involved in a small group that teaches the Word.

The point of reading along with others is that we can misunderstand things when we're on our own, but we're more likely to sort out our misunderstandings if we read with others. In a small group we may have the added benefit of a Bible study guide that explains things like the definitions of words and the cultural background of events. God never intended for us to be off on our own trying to figure everything out. We do have the Holy Spirit to guide us, but He often speaks through other people.

As Usual

I hope you realize it's also vital to spend time in prayer each morning before you walk out the door. How much time does it take you to get ready for your day? If it takes thirty minutes, then get up thirty minutes earlier, throw on your Holy Spirit clothes, and eat your Jesus breakfast. I am convinced we as Christians don't pray enough. We certainly can't pray *too much*, if you think about it! Have you ever gotten up from a time of prayer and thought, *Well, I just prayed too much today*. No, I can almost guarantee no one has ever said that and meant it.

Yet when Jesus walked this earth, it was common for Him to be found praying to the Father. Luke 22:39 says, "Jesus went out as usual to the Mount of Olives . . ." *As usual.* I bet the disciples pretty much always knew where they could find Jesus, especially first thing in the morning or at the end of the day. Jesus often said things like, "I only do what I see the Father doing," (see John 5:19) and "I only say what the Father tells me to say" (see John 12:49). To do what the Father was doing, He had to choose each and every day to stop and see what the Father was doing. And to say what the Father told Him to say, He had to be listening to what the Father was saying to Him.

One of many things I love and appreciate about my wife, Michelle, is that I have never worried about where she is spiritually. Every single morning Michelle gets up early, makes a cup of coffee (decaf! Why bother?), and spends time in the Word and prayer. I always know where to find her, because she always sits in the same place. *As usual.* I don't remember ever praying for Michelle to fall in love with God again. She can't say the same about me, I guarantee it! She had to pray that for me during a time when I had fallen out of love with God.

I remember when the Lord was stirring my heart to move to Arkansas. I was afraid of it and desired to get out of ministry. I just wanted to run. Michelle was quite concerned, and rightly so, that I was going to go off track into a business venture, leaving ministry for good. She got on the phone and called all of her friends and told them, "Rick is about to make the worst decision of his life." She was seeking the Lord for me, and I am thankful for that.

Listen Well

An active, engaged prayer life involves *listening well.* Jesus told His disciples, "I do nothing on my own but say only what the Father taught me. And the one who sent me is with me—he has not deserted me" (John 8:28–29 NLT). The only way Jesus could do what the Father told Him to do was if He listened!

Ninety percent of climbers who attempt to climb to the summit of Mount Everest fail, and 165 have died trying since 1953. So when Erik Weihenmayer reached Mount Everest's summit on May 25, 2001, that was amazing in itself. What makes Erik's climb even more amazing is that he has been blind since he was thirteen. Why did he succeed? Because he listened well. He listened for a bell tied to the back of the climber in front of him. He listened for instructions from teammates who would shout directions to him. He listened for the sound of his pick jabbing the ice so he would know whether it was safe to cross. The more you listen for God's voice in your prayer life, the more you will actually hear it. And the more you hear what He is saying, the more likely you'll be to follow in His footsteps and the more acutely you'll know how to respond to the world around you.

Pray for discernment. Pray for it every day. Then listen to what God wants to get through to you. Listen to the Scriptures and listen to the wise people God has put in your life.

Conclusion

The Bible is the story of God, the story of how He extends real love to hurting people and connects people together so they can show real love to one another. From the beginning, the story unfolds as a series of covenants—promises between God and His people.

As you begin to move through what might be a new or deeper understanding of real love, my prayer is that this revelation begins changing how you relate to those in the world around you.

4

The Heart of God

When I was a kid, I would try anything. My friends and I often made ramps for our bikes to see how far we could jump. One particular day, I had just jumped about five feet in the air, so I thought I was Evel Knievel! My friend's dad had a Volkswagen, so with kid swagger I told my friend, "If you can get the keys to your dad's car, I will build a ramp and jump over it!" He agreed, and my friends built the ramp while I strategized over the plan. The biggest challenge, in my mind, was building up enough speed to get over the van. So I decided to hold on to another kid while he drove his motorbike toward the ramp.

Everything seemed perfect. And then, in midair, my front tire came off. It's hard to land with no front tire. It's even more challenging when the front frame forks stick into the ground. My friends probably would have helped sooner, but they were laughing so hard that they couldn't walk over to me. I laughed too . . . some weeks later. It's amazing any of us lived through childhood.

When you were a kid, did you ever have *two* really close friends at the same time? When three kids are close friends, it's not unusual for one of them to feel left out. It happens often enough that we have a name for the person who doesn't quite fit: the third wheel. But beginning in Genesis and continuing throughout the Word, we read over and over again a consistent description of a relationship of perfect unity, complete oneness between three "persons."

Right from the start, the Bible portrays God's character as wrapped in a covenant relationship. Genesis 1:1 reads, "In the beginning, *God* . . ." The Hebrew word in this verse for "God" is *Elohim*, a plural noun. This God speaks everything into existence, hovers over the waters, and walks in the Garden in the cool of the morning. It's a plural noun, but it refers to a unified being who does everything with one mind and heart.

What is going on here? The Bible is offering a huge clue about who our God is: He is one-in-three and three-in-one. He is God, singular, portrayed in a perfect, unified *relationship* of three. He is the "Trinity"—three persons in one, perfectly distinct and yet altogether one.

Hints like these are found throughout the Old Testament. In the New Testament, this three-person God is identified as Father, Son, and Holy Spirit. Before God created the world, the Father, the Son, and the Holy Spirit shared a perfect relationship of real love. Out of that relationship, God created the world and human beings, and now He reaches out to us in love to restore broken people. Once we experience the real love of God, we can share it with others.

In John 5:19, Jesus tells the Jewish leaders He "can do only what he sees his Father doing, because whatever the Father does the Son also does." Later, in John 12:50, Jesus says, "Whatever I say is just what the Father has told me to say." At one level, Jesus is explaining His unique relationship with the Father here. They are perfectly united in vision and values. At another level, though, Jesus is modeling how all of us learn to live the way God calls us to live. We learn by watching and listening to the Father. If we want to know how to demonstrate real love in an angry world, we have to pay attention to the Father.

The Best Relationship Ever

When we started New Life Church, we constantly reminded people that our focus was to "love God, love people, and love life." We didn't make up the first two points in that mission statement. When the Pharisees asked Jesus to list the greatest commandment in the law, He told them, "Love the Lord your God with all your heart and with all your soul and with all your mind" (Matt. 22:37). He added, "And the second is like it: 'Love your neighbor as yourself'" (v. 39). This is not brand-new information for most people.

But the last part of our mission statement may surprise you—God actually wants us to *enjoy* loving Him and loving others. Keeping those "greatest commandments" isn't supposed to be a drag. That's why we remind our congregation to "love life." Loving God and loving your neighbor should be a blast! But what does that look like in day-to-day relationships? How do we set the tone and develop open, friendly, and authentic relationships? The secret is in the word *covenant*.

Covenant is a fancy word for "agreement." The God of the Bible is a covenant-making God. That means God makes promises and keeps them. He pursues relationships with flawed, sinful people. And He wants us to love one another the way He loves us. He wants us to pursue relationships with one another and keep our promises. It all starts with God, as we meet Him in His Word. The way He reaches out to people in their need shows us what real love looks like.

God's Covenant with Noah

The first time the Bible mentions the word *covenant* is in Genesis 6, when God initiated a relationship with Noah. God basically said, "Hey, Noah, I promise I will never again destroy the earth by flood." It's a commitment God made by His own initiative, and God will always do what He says He will do. We still see rainbows today as the sign of God's promise to Noah, because His commitment to Noah and *all generations* is still in effect. To God, "never" means *never*. Everyone living today is a descendant of Noah, so we are all covered with a promise founded on a relationship God established with one man thousands of years ago. I don't know about you, but I've never kept a promise that long!

This story shows us that God is eager to be in relationship with us. He wants to be around *you*, me, and all His people! He wants to be around us so much, in fact, that He goes out of His way to commit Himself to us, to make promises He intends to keep forever. Real love is like that. It doesn't blow with the changing wind. It's a promise that stays consistent.

God's Covenant with Abraham

Hundreds of years passed between when God made His covenant with Noah and the moment He reached out to a man named Abram and invited him to leave his hometown, Haran. Out of the blue, God said to Abram,

> Leave your native country, your relatives, and your father's family, and go to the land that I will show you. I will make you into a great nation. I will bless you and make you famous, and you will be a blessing to others. I will bless those who bless you and curse those who treat you with contempt. All the families on earth will be blessed through you (Gen. 12:1–3 NLT).

Hear those promises? "*I* will make you a great nation." "*I* will bless you." God was making promises and not asking much from Abram. And because Abraham listened and obeyed, the two entered a covenant agreement.

When God started a relationship with Abram, Abram picked up a new name. He became "Abraham . . . the friend of God" (James 2:23 NLT). God took on a new nickname too. From then on God referred to Himself as the "God of Abraham, Isaac, and Jacob" (Exod. 3:16). With that nickname, God was reminding everybody *He* chose to associate with *this man* and his descendants. God was saying, "You don't get one of us without the other. I've got Abraham's back."

And just like God gave Noah the rainbow as a sign of their covenant, God gave Abraham a sign too. The sign for Abraham was circumcision. If I had been Abraham, I would have been mad about that. He must have thought, *Wait a minute! How'd I get circumcision? I want a rainbow!*

Over time, God spoke numerous promises to Abraham, including promises to bless him and give him many descendants who would bring blessing to the whole earth. The only way all this could have happened was if God made it happen. God showed real love by taking responsibility for their relationship. All Abraham had to do was listen and obey. God promised to take care of the rest.

God's Covenant with Moses

Centuries passed between Abraham and Moses. Just before Moses is introduced in Exodus 2, we discover that Abraham's descendants, the Israelites, were enslaved in Egypt. When God heard their cries for help, "He remembered his covenant with Abraham, with Isaac and with Jacob" (Exod. 2:24), and He acted on it. When the Bible says He "remembered," that doesn't mean the promises He had made had slipped His mind and then popped back into it one day. It means God delivered the Israelites from Egypt on the basis of a promise He had made to Abraham hundreds of years before! Real love acts.

After God rescued the Israelites from bondage in Egypt, things took a new turn. Up to this point, God's promises had been about His relationship with people—vertical relationships, in a sense. Beginning with Moses, we see that God is concerned about His relationship with us, His people, *and* our relationships with one another. We usually emphasize our relationship with God and undervalue our relationships with one another, but God is concerned about both.

The Ten Commandments (see Exod. 20) summarize how God wants people to love Him and one another. They include some dos (remember the Sabbath and honor your parents) and some don'ts (don't steal, don't kill, and so on). God is still reaching out in love. But real love always has boundaries. Relationships are always a choice. God is not a dictator. We get to live wherever we want to live, and we get to choose whatever we want to choose. Many of those decisions have significant consequences, such as spending eternity outside of God's presence. But we are free to choose. The day Moses came down Mount Sinai and delivered the commandments, the Israelites responded wholeheartedly, "We will do *everything* the LORD has said" (Exod. 19:8, emphasis added).

I'm so glad God gave us boundaries as we learned to relate to Him and to those around us. I'm so glad He gave us the law to teach us how to live. I joke around sometimes about effective and ineffective parenting techniques. One technique is teaching from experience. It goes something like this: "Okay, little Johnny. You are now four years old, and today we're going to learn about burners. Just take your finger and put it right there on the stove. See how hot that is? That's right. Now you know not to do that again. Okay, now come over here to the outlet and stick your finger right there in that hole. Feel that? That's right. That's electricity. Now you know not to do that. Tomorrow we're going to learn about traffic." How horrible would God be if He taught us this way?

When you're a child in God's house, He expects you to live a certain way. But instead of our figuring out how to live by trial and error, He gives us the law. Proverbs 4:1 says, "Listen, my sons, to a father's instruction." The Lord wants us to listen to His instruction and choose to live within the boundaries He has in place for us. He does this to keep us safe.

Since my dad nearly died last year, my conversations with him are now different. I went to Israel recently, but before I left, my dad said, "I don't want you to go to Israel." Instead of plowing ahead like I used to do, I asked him, "Are you telling me not to go?" I needed to hear him out. Now, I don't think we have to *obey* our parents the rest of our lives, but the Bible says to *honor* our father and mother. One way to honor them is to listen.

"I'm not telling you not to go," Dad responded. "I just love you. I just want you to be safe."

Not all instructions are the same. When my kids were young, there were times when they were running out the door and I told them things like, "Hey! Don't forget your shoes!" or "Close the door behind you!" Those things are not really that important.

But there were other times when I grabbed them, looked them in the eyes, and warned them, "Stop playing in the street. It is going to kill you." I once told my oldest son, Hunter, "Stop beating up your brother and sister. Do you want me to do to *you* what I did to your older brother?"

"But Dad, I don't *have* an older brother," Hunter responded.

"See?!" I said.

In these moments, when your child's safety is on the line, you know they have to get it, they have to clearly understand what you're saying—it's at these times that your instructions can have an edge to them. I'm no prophet, that's for sure, but the Word of God has a prophetic edge to it. It warns us to pay attention.

When the people of Israel *promised* they would do everything the Lord commanded, it was a noble thought, but it was an empty promise. That never happened. Quite literally, while God was explaining the covenant boundaries to Moses, the Israelites were wandering off, creating an idol, and worshiping it. Despite the Israelites' behavior, God kept going, starting with the most essential instructions—the Ten Commandments. The first four are about our relationship with God, while the remainder are about our relationships with one another. They are all important, but the order is also important. It's necessary to get the most important relationship settled first—our relationship with God—before we try and develop deep connections with other people.

In other words, we can't give real love to others unless we are experiencing real love with God. If we want deep connections with other people, we must first be in a deep relationship with God. Why? Because in that relationship with Him, He changes us to *be like Him* through the power of the Holy Spirit in our hearts, the presence of God in our lives. Without the Holy Spirit, the change is unsustainable. And the way we relate with people is a direct reflection of how close we truly are to God.

Trusting the God of the Covenants

Sometimes we shy away from God because we have a warped perspective of who He really is. If we think God is mad at us, we won't choose to be around Him, because we believe He doesn't really want to be around us. Or we think He's just sitting around waiting to punish us for something.

I remember one time my son Tanner was in a golf tournament in high school. It was a tough day for him; he wasn't doing well. I knew what would help him, but the rules kept me from being able to say anything to him. So I just sat there, frustrated that I couldn't help and sad for what was happening to him.

Once he teed up and shanked the ball on the opening drive. I rolled my eyes, irritated that I couldn't say anything to him. I couldn't give advice, support, or encouragement. Nothing was allowed. But the real problem was that he looked over at me just as I rolled my eyes.

I immediately thought, *Oh no! Tanner thinks I'm mad at him, and when this game is over, he's not going to want to be around me. He won't want to be in relationship with me.* After the game, I found out that was exactly what he was thinking and how he felt. I'm so glad I noticed that he noticed my eye-rolling, because that moment could have destroyed him. It could have destroyed our relationship, had I not been paying attention.

First John 3:1 promises us this: "See what great love the Father has lavished on us, that we should be called children of God! And that is what we are!" We grow when we trust that the God who makes covenants loves us and is for us. Just as Tanner was that day on the golf course, we'll be tempted to give up if we think our heavenly Father is angry with us or fed up with us. If you don't take anything else from this chapter, hear this: God loves you. He isn't angry with you. He wants what's best for you. He has proven that over and over again by the way He reaches out in love.

The New Covenant

After four hundred years of silence between the Old and New Testaments, Jesus took real love to a whole new level. In the final week of His ministry, He simplified the entire

Old Testament when He essentially said, "Love God first and love your neighbors like yourself." He then walked through fulfilling every promise God ever made with humankind, not because He was forced to, but because He wanted to. In His life, He showed us what real love looks like.

Jesus also showed us real love in His death on the cross. Right before He was crucified, He and His disciples were sharing the Passover meal together. He had just washed His disciples' feet, foretold His own betrayal, commanded Judas to carry out his plan to betray Him, and predicted Peter's denial. Jesus had one final meal to tell His disciples the most important things in His heart before He left. In those final moments, He talked to them about real love and true friendship.

Jesus stopped the meal, held up some bread, broke it apart, and said, "This is my body given for you." He lifted a cup of wine and said, "This cup is the *new* covenant in *my blood*, which is *poured out* for you" (Luke 22:19–20, emphasis added). The disciples were probably confused at first, because Jesus went off script. The Israelites had been doing Passover for hundreds of years. The disciples had done it every year for their entire lives. They had to have been thinking, *What's Jesus doing? This isn't how the Passover meal is supposed to work!* It suddenly dawned on the disciples that He had just said the word *covenant* when He talked about pouring out His own blood. That moment was not lost on them; they fully understood the meaning of the term. They knew He was about to fulfill God's promises and open the door to begin a new covenant. They didn't know exactly *how* He was going to do it, but they knew something important was going down.

Then, within just a few hours, the disciples learned that real love hurts. Sometimes real love breaks your heart. The Bible says, "God made him who had no sin to be sin for us" (2 Cor. 5:21). In the moment of His crucifixion, Jesus Himself became the sacrifice of the covenant, and the moment He gave up His spirit, the huge temple veil that kept people out of the presence of God was ripped in half—top to bottom. This symbolized the body of Christ being torn for us, making the way for us to enter the throne room of God, enabling us to relate to Him directly.

Right before He went to the cross, Jesus said, "No longer do I call you servants . . . but I have called you friends" (John 15:15 ESV). Then almost the first thing He said to Mary Magdalene after He came up out of the grave was, "Go instead to my *brothers* and tell them, 'I am ascending to my Father and your Father, to my God and your God'" (John 20:17, emphasis added). When Jesus gave His life, He opened the door so we can be not just friends of God, but His family—His sons and daughters. Going forward, the new covenant promises that you can have a brand-new relationship with Him, and He gives you access to everything He has. Essentially, Jesus promises, "From this point forward, you have the right and the power to ask for anything in My name and I will do it for you. Call on My name if you need a miracle. You are part of My family, and I will show up."

Both before and after the resurrection, Jesus spoke numerous *promises* to the disciples—He promised to always be with them and to prepare a place for them, He declared Himself the way to the Father, and He promised to send a helper. God was saying, "I've got your back! Everything I have is yours. I give you My word. I will never leave you."

This is what God said to Noah and Abraham and Moses. Now He's saying it to us too. Because we've seen God make good on these promises all through the Bible, we can trust them. Real love isn't just words. Real love keeps its promises.

This Is Kind of a Big Deal

When Jesus died on the cross, He became the sacrifice for our sin, making it possible for us to have a relationship with God. But He did more than that. Most of the time when we talk about the new covenant, we talk only about how Jesus's death on the cross makes us right with God. That's great news! But there's even more good news. Jesus's death and resurrection make us right with God and make it possible for us to live in right relationship with others.

This isn't a hidden lesson. Jesus was always talking about the way His followers should love one another in a way people just couldn't (or wouldn't!) wrap their brains around. He said things like, "Serve one another" (Gal. 5:13); "If you want to live, you have to be willing to die" (see Rom. 8:13); and "If you want to be first, you have to be willing to be last" (see Mark 9:35). This is an upside-down kingdom. Jesus didn't come to be served, but to serve (see Matt. 20:28). Jesus showed real love in His life and death, and His resurrection makes it possible for us to show real love to others.

Jesus told His disciples,

> As the Father has loved me, so have I loved you. Now remain in my love. If you keep my commands, you will remain in my love, just as I have kept my Father's commands and remain in his love. I have told you this so that my joy may be in you

and that your joy may be complete. My command is this: Love each other as I have loved you. Greater love has no one than this: to lay down one's life for one's friends. You are my friends if you do what I command. I no longer call you servants, because a servant does not know his master's business. Instead, I have called you friends, for everything that I learned from my Father I have made known to you. You did not choose me, but I chose you and appointed you so that you might go and bear fruit—fruit that will last—and so that whatever you ask in my name the Father will give you. This is my command: Love each other. (John 15:9–17)

Because of what Jesus accomplished, and because God poured out His Holy Spirit when the church was born, things that mattered before don't matter anymore. It doesn't matter if you are born free or enslaved. It doesn't matter if you are young or old. It doesn't matter if you are rich or poor. Jesus's family doesn't have entry requirements. He brought people in from every nation, tribe, walk, and status to do life with one another differently. It was a new model for life, a new family devoted to one another.

Conclusion

Jesus gives us the power to be victorious in our relationships. He promises us His weapons to fight our enemies. And God's Word makes it clear who the enemy is and who it isn't. Paul says this in Ephesians 6:10–12:

A final word: Be strong in the Lord and in his mighty power. Put on all of God's armor so that you will be able to stand firm against all strategies of the devil. For we are not fighting

against flesh-and-blood enemies, but against evil rulers and
authorities of the unseen world, against mighty powers in
this dark world, and against evil spirits in the heavenly places.
(NLT)

Friends, we get this wrong too often. One reason the
world doesn't know what real love looks like is because the
church has viewed the world as the enemy. That's one reason
the world is angry! They don't know real love because we
haven't shown it to them. We talk about love, but what we
demonstrate is hate. We talk about winning them to Jesus
with our words, but our actions make it clear we think we're
at war with the culture around us. Unbelievers are not the
enemy. The enemy is the devil, who keeps the world blind
and scared and broken. Unbelievers are the people Jesus is
asking us to reach out to with real, tough, sacrificial, selfless
love. They are the people He died for! He's asking us to go
get them and bring them in.

Our secret weapon is relationships. Focus on how Jesus
set the example for us with His disciples.

One of the first things Jesus did when He got back together
with the disciples after His resurrection was to meet them
while they were fishing. He then cooked the fish and served it
to His friends. Through His actions, Jesus was saying, "You
don't have to go to the temple first; the relationship I have
with you is the same as the kind you have with your friends.
This is how we do life. Real love is living life together."

Unfortunately, the new model of life Jesus calls us to follow
is becoming a thing of the past. The kind of relationship Jesus
wants us to have with one another is increasingly difficult
to find. Jesus told the disciples the world would know they

were His disciples by the way they loved one another (John 13:34). Real love is our strongest testimony. If we don't love one another the way Jesus intended, then the world won't know we are believers. It won't matter what we say if our actions don't communicate our commitment to Jesus and one another. If we testify to Jesus in an angry world, we have to learn to love the way God intended. If our God is a covenant-making God, then as His children we should be covenant-making people. If people matter so much to God that He pursues them and initiates permanent relationships with them, then we have to do the same thing. How? Keep reading.

5

Learning How to Agree Again

For as long as I can remember, I wanted to be able to drive. I remember even at five years old, I wanted to drive. My parents weren't open to that. When I was eight, I begged them to let me learn. They still didn't agree.

When I was twelve, my grandfather died and our family inherited his vehicle. Our driveway was forty feet long, so my mom let me drive in that driveway. I would floor it right toward the fence and then slam on the brakes, barely stopping before the fence. Then I'd put the car in reverse and floor it back to the road. I went up and down the driveway every day. I learned to work that clutch! It was an old Ford Falcon, and I nicknamed it "Kan-Hartly," because it could roll up one hill but "Kan-Hartly" get up the next one! It was a horrible car. Everything about it was broken.

Someone who drives a new car probably takes better care of it than the way I took care of that old Ford Falcon. You take care of the things you value. When you value someone as much as you value yourself, you treat them differently than if you valued them as an object, servant, or stepping-stone. And when you realize how highly Jesus values others (He died for them too, not just for you!), it will fundamentally affect how you treat them, both within and outside the body of Christ. If people matter to Jesus, then they should matter to you. To learn how to live out God's love in an angry world, you have to know how to navigate among people, through relational challenges and difficulties. Of course, first you have to actually care about other people. If you "Kan-Hartly" care about them, then you're never going to enjoy covenant relationships.

What Is Real Love Anyway?

The kinds of relationships Jesus wants us to have in the body of Christ are covenant relationships. These are relationships of real love made possible only because of the work Jesus accomplished on the cross. They give us opportunities to live in a more connected way with others, a connectedness that is fiercely needed in our culture today. There are so many dysfunctional families these days that people can't count on their own parents or siblings for any kind of support. It saddens me to the core. People need real friends because so many of them don't have real families anymore.

In the early church there was a season when real love flourished and was clearly demonstrated. Check out Acts 2:42–47 (Message):

> They committed themselves to the teaching of all the apostles, the life together, the common meal, and the prayers.

Everyone around was in awe—all those wonders and signs done through the apostles! All the believers lived in a wonderful harmony, holding everything in common. They sold whatever they owned and pooled their resources so that each person's need was met. They followed a daily discipline of worship in the Temple followed by meals at home, every meal a celebration, exuberant and joyful, as they praised God. People in general liked what they saw. Every day their number grew as God added those who were saved.

This almost sounds like some kind of strange utopian existence, doesn't it? I believe this is true simply because we live in a culture that has been driven by materialism, humanism, pride, top-down leadership, and me-first attitudes for generations! Acts 2 describes a community of believers who *freely chose* to love one another, put others first, and meet one another's needs because they *wanted to*, not because they *had to*. That's as clear a picture of a supportive Christian community, an extended family of faith, as you'll ever see.

This is one of the reasons Jesus died—so we could experience this community. That would be reason enough to make it a priority! But there's more. I believe these relationships are a more effective way to win people into the kingdom of God than by arguing and debating. The Bible backs me up on this.

You're probably familiar with the first part of 1 Peter 3:15, which says, "Always be prepared to give an answer to everyone who asks you to give the reason for the hope that you have." But the verse doesn't end there. It actually keeps going on to say, "But do this with gentleness and respect." Well, guess what? The sentence still doesn't end there! It actually continues into verse 16, which reads, "Keeping a clear conscience, so that those who speak maliciously against your good behavior in Christ may be ashamed of their slander."

I like the way *The Message* translates this passage. Check this out:

> Be ready to speak up and tell anyone who asks why you're living the way you are, and always with the utmost courtesy. Keep a clear conscience before God so that when people throw mud at you, none of it will stick. They'll end up realizing that *they're* the ones who need a bath. It's better to suffer for doing good, if that's what God wants, than to be punished for doing bad.

The Bible is incredible at teaching tact, common courtesy, and how to have favor with others! It's the best book anywhere for developing your people skills. Did you notice the balance in the Word? If we pay attention to only the first part, then we may be ready to talk about why we believe what we believe, why we follow Christ, and why we believe the Bible is true. In other words, we may get ready for a fight. But that's not what the Word asks us to do. The second half of that passage basically says, "Wait! Before answering their question, don't forget that *how* you say what you say is just as important as *what* you say."

It's common in our culture to feel like we're forced to take sides on every issue. Some people believe it is their duty in life to go on Facebook and broadcast their gift of revelation about what is right and wrong. Some of those convictions are from God, and others may not be, but that's not the point. The point is that your convictions should never be broadcast. They have to be requested.

The Greek word for "give an answer" in 1 Peter 3:15 is *apologia*, which implies being subpoenaed. Living your ordinary, day-to-day life in a godly way in full view of others is infinitely more powerful than going on social media to say, "We just want to make sure you know we're antigay." Good grief, don't do that. When someone invites you into their home and culture, you then have permission to speak into their lives. If they haven't embraced you or they don't allow you to embrace them, then you don't have the right to speak. It's not game time yet. Wait until your convictions are requested.

Let me be clear. I am *not* saying that we shouldn't assess situations with wisdom or make value judgments. We have to use wisdom to navigate this world, and it's important to live within the boundaries God has placed for us. When we do that, we live within God's blessing. What I *am* saying is that as we communicate, as we relate to others, we need to be careful to eliminate the critical spirit and ratchet down the anger.

Take gay marriage, for example. Some people totally affirm every decision the US government is sending down the pipeline, while others hold up protest signs that read "God Hates Fags" and march around on the sidewalk yelling at everybody. Before you know it, a reporter is shoving a microphone in your face, asking which side you're on.

Usually when I speak about a controversial issue, I bring up problems with both sides of the issue. It's important to understand how and why people who are polarized by an issue feel the way they feel, and it's important to weave in your perspective of wisdom, conviction, and responsibility rather than judgment toward their position. This applies to both extremes of controversial issues. The biblical response to one side of the gay marriage issue is clear—God designed marriage to be between a man and a woman. And the biblical response to the other side of the gay marriage issue is equally clear—we are called to walk side by side with others in their journey for truth.

Real love maintains the boundaries God has placed around our lives, while using wisdom to navigate tough conversations. On a practical level, when I'm in a tough conversation with someone whose position on a subject is directly contrary to God's boundaries, I sincerely try to understand how they feel. Then I turn the conversation, with honor for the other person, toward what I have found to be true in my relationship with God. If I lose the relationship (and we all do sometimes), it better not be because of the way I have treated the other person! On the flip side, if I have kept a friend in the process, it better be because I've chosen to treat them with respect, not because I've chosen to acquiesce to their ideas. Real love leads with kindness while honoring God's boundaries.

Laying Down Our Lives

Jesus challenged His disciples with a clear definition of real love: "Greater love has no one than this, that one lay down his life for his friends" (John 15:13 NASB).

We can read this verse as a challenge to die for others. On rare occasions we might actually have to give our life for a friend. More often, though, the application of this command to "lay down your life" is to set aside your own priorities, your own goals and ambitions, and go help out a brother or sister.

Here's an example of how this works. A friend of mine was recently shopping for a car. He and his wife have a goal of being debt-free, so they were challenged to find a reliable car in a reasonable price range (sounds like everybody!). Well, that friend had another friend who purchased a newer car around the same time. Instead of trading or reselling their old car, they agreed to sell it to my friend for a fair and reasonable price. Now my friend has a reliable car and should have it paid off long before this book goes to print. This transaction came about because these two people are in a network of real relationships. They know each other's needs, they pray for each other, and they share with joy as they are willing and able.

A member of one of our church's small groups had health issues. His son, who also had health issues and was financially strapped, needed to move to a different apartment that was easier for him to get in and out of. Basically, he needed to move from a third-floor apartment (a lot of stairs) to a ground-floor apartment. The father asked his small group if anyone would be willing to help his son move. The following weekend, ten strong men joyfully moved this young man to his new home in fewer than two hours.

This doesn't sound like earth-shattering stuff. It really isn't. Everyone wants to get as much money as they can for their used car. And everyone has plans on Saturday. But when people are in covenant with one another, their priorities change and what is most important is meeting the needs of a person they really love.

So how does this affect how we live in an angry world? Look at this amazing prayer Jesus prayed just before His crucifixion:

The goal is for all of them to become one heart and mind—just as you, Father, are in me and I in you, so they might be one heart and mind with us. Then the world might believe that you, in fact, sent me. The same glory you gave me, I gave them, so they'll be as unified and together as we are—I in them and you in me. Then they'll be mature in this oneness, and give the godless world evidence that you've sent me and loved them in the same way you've loved me. (John 17:20–23 Message)

Whoa! Did you catch what Jesus says is at stake in our relationships? When Christians live out real love in their relationships, the world outside the church will recognize God sent Jesus and He loves everyone! A lot is riding on our relationships. As we are unified in His Spirit, we demonstrate to the world how much God loves us—and *how much God loves the world.*

People tell me all the time they are praying and asking God to bring revival to our nation and to transform our culture. I am certainly all for our nation returning to God. Yet Jesus prayed for us to have unity in the Spirit, which would then result in a demonstration to the world of how much God loves us. What? We're praying for God to move, and God is waiting on us to learn how to get along! Could it possibly be that God will bring revival to the lost in our nation when they see that we love one another and actually care about *them?*

Real Love Is a Choice

Just as being in relationship with Jesus Christ is something we choose, the difference between real love and its substitutes is choice. Most relationships, including too many marriages, are based on feelings alone. When the relationship feels good and makes us happy, when it's easy and rewarding, we keep it. When challenges get even more challenging, or when the relationship doesn't feel good anymore, we drop it. That's not real love. It's real when we choose to be in relationship with people.

Michelle and I have chosen to be in covenant with a handful of friends we know from our ministry work. I even told the men, "If anything were ever to happen to you, we'll take care of your wife for the rest of her life. It will never be okay with us for someone to say something negative about you to us. We have your back, and we will be there for you. I'm asking you to do the same for us, because we're in covenant with you."

That may sound extreme, so here's a more everyday example of what real love looks like.

I spent a significant amount of time in my youth smoking marijuana. When I first gave my heart to the Lord in 1981, I initially stopped doing it, but later I noticed that I wanted it again. I didn't really know what to do, because I knew it could destroy me. Thankfully, I had also just gotten involved in a church where I knew someone—my uncle Randall. So I told him about it. With simple truth, I said, "Hey, I feel like if I ever had a chance to smoke pot again without anybody knowing it, I would do it."

I was surprised when he responded, "Well, you've already won half the battle, because you told somebody. So let's pray about it, and I will keep on checking in with you."

After that, at least two or three times a week, he called to check on me. For a whole year, I kept praying through it, and he kept checking on me. One day, as I was driving to Atlanta,

I stopped for gas. When I got out of the car I dropped my keys on the ground. When I reached down to pick them up, I saw that they had landed right on top of a joint. So I picked up the keys, and then I picked up the joint. My first thought was, *Thank you, Lord! God is good!*

I got back in the car and punched in the cigarette lighter. I rolled down the window and put the joint in my mouth. But before the lighter popped out, I remembered my uncle who had encouraged me for an entire year, knowing he would check on me and see if I was all right. That thought gave me the strength to throw the joint out the window.

I'll tell you what saved me—I was connected. I was in a real relationship with my uncle Randall, though I didn't know at the time that's what it was.

Second Corinthians 4:2 (Message) says, "We refuse to wear masks and play games. We don't maneuver and manipulate behind the scenes. . . . Rather, we keep everything we do and say out in the open." We can't be 100 percent open with everybody—that would be extreme—but with believers who care, we live candidly and honestly. At New Life Church, I'm certainly glad we're growing larger, but I'm only interested if we can grow smaller at the same time. I'm interested not in a shallow or weak church, but a place where people are in the Word and connected in relationships in which we check on one another.

This is not how most relationships work. Most of the time, when we don't feel it anymore, we either quit the relationship or lose our sense of security with the other person. That's a relationship based on feelings, not commitment.

When you're in a real relationship with other believers, what does that actually look like? How does that affect how you treat one another and how you treat people in the culture around you? Though we don't have Old Testament rituals to walk through anymore, the agreement is still just as strong: we choose to honor, respect, trust, maintain integrity, commit to fight for one another, and be there for one another.

Real Love Covers Others

People in covenant relationship with one another are challenged and encouraged to cover one another. But what does it mean to "cover" one another? It simply means that we choose to honor them publicly. A simple way to honor publicly is by supporting the other person, letting them know we are with them, we are for them, we've got their back. We may not agree with everything they say or do, but there is a time and a place for hashing that out. That place and time is *privately* and *later*. We'll talk about that in a bit.

Real love covers weaknesses and emphasizes strengths. When someone's weaknesses become the topic of conversation, it is important to quickly redirect the conversation to their strengths. You don't know what that person can do with God's Spirit in them, so speak to their strengths! Always be on board with the other person. Always choose to believe the best and speak the best about them. Especially behind their back. It's what we would want, right? Let me provide an example of how this plays out sometimes.

At New Life Church, we have a goal of reaching the entire state of Arkansas with the message that God loves people and so do we, that Jesus died to not only save them but also to bring them new life on planet Earth. I have covenant relationships with all our pastors and staff. When we plant a campus in a new city, we usually send teams of pastors and leaders who feel called to that city and are prepared to lead. Sometimes word leaks out about who those people are. Sometimes, but certainly not always, I get feedback from others that sounds something like this: "Why did you choose *him* to be the worship pastor (or campus pastor or whatever)?" And occasionally, if the person saying it is really bold (or unwise), that comment might be followed up with some kind of critique of the pastor's skills or maturity level. Why does this happen? People criticize others for numerous reasons. Maybe they simply haven't submitted the way they communicate and the words they choose to the control of the Holy Spirit. Usually the situation is more complicated. Usually there's something about that person that makes them feel insecure or maybe even jealous about the choices we have made.

I'd be the first to admit that sometimes we don't make the right call and someone gets into a position they're just not ready for. I'll admit that, but what I *won't do* is buy into the negativity. If the truth be known, none of us is ever as prepared as we could be for the calling that God has on our lives. But that doesn't mean I agree with the critics. It also doesn't mean I have the right to be negative back to a negative person. Adding negativity doesn't help.

Here's what I do when someone complains to me about one of our church staff members: I redirect the content of the conversation in a way that honors the team *and* the complaining person. My main goal is to fully support our team, because that negative person is in the wrong for speaking badly of someone behind their back.

People have to know that it's okay to be frustrated. When a church member has legitimate concerns or complaints, of course I listen to them. If one of my close friends hurts someone, I'm not going to let them get away with it just because we're in covenant together. But real love covers others. And that means I will not join in when others are speaking badly about someone. Jesus talked about how to handle situations like this. He said, "If another believer sins against you, go privately and point out the offense" (Matt. 18:15 NLT). When we do it this way, the relationship is preserved. Jesus added, "If the other person listens and confesses it, you have won that person back." So that's what I expect from covenant relationship. If someone truly has an issue with a person we have chosen as a leader or pastor, they learn to handle it by going directly to that person and/or their own overseer about it. Honestly, it usually doesn't come to that.

Real love chooses to approach all relationship problems privately and directly. Don't walk around pretending your relationship doesn't have any problems. But there is a time and place to address issues. Don't spout your frustration with everyone *except* the person you have a problem with! When you have a problem with someone, choose not to share the problem with five other people before going to the person you need to talk to about it. Be honest with them, but do it with honor and wisdom.

It's important to honor others, whether it's your spouse, your employer, your employees, your neighbors, or even those in government. Simply table the conversation—and the emotion—and come back to it when you're in a private setting. When you demonstrate loyalty and honor in public, you'll have favor with the other person if you have hard things to say behind closed doors.

Real Love Leads with Kindness

Supporting someone publicly and choosing to emphasize the positive doesn't mean you never call someone out for their sin. It doesn't mean anything goes. An important part of real love is confrontation. But loving someone changes the way you confront them. Real love leads with kindness.

When I lived in Louisiana, I had a healthy group of friends, but one of them decided to separate from his wife and have an affair. A judgmental response would have been to shame him, make him feel bad, or get in his face and call him a dirtbag. That's what I, and the rest of my group of friends, wanted to do. To be honest, half of us wanted to hurt him. *He should know better*, we thought.

The "sloppy agape" response would have been to say something like, "It's okay, bro. We all make mistakes. Let's have a beer and not talk about it." Or "I've never seen you this happy; I know how hard it is to be married. You deserve to be happy." None of us wanted to do that.

We knew his behavior pattern. He regularly met this woman on Friday nights. We talked extensively about how we should respond. Finally, someone in the group came up with a great idea. We would hang out in his front yard on Friday nights until he got home. We agreed that we wouldn't yell at him or even give him condescending looks, but that we would just be kind to him and let him know we loved him.

The next Friday night, he came home sometime around 3:00 a.m., and there we all were—sitting in lawn chairs in his front yard. He came stumbling up to the door and we quietly said what we had agreed to say: "We love you, man. We just want to be there for you. Let us know if there's anything we can do." He didn't say anything back though. He just went inside. We waited a little while, and then we packed up and went home. Sometimes you just need to let people know, with kindness, that you care about them. Sometimes you don't need to directly address the problem they're facing—at least not yet.

The following Friday night, we did the same thing. Week after week, we continued. Not too long into it, he came home, fell on his knees right there in the front yard, and cried like a baby. Shame didn't get to him and yelling wouldn't have reached him. Love did. Consistent love met him—reaching out to him right where he was—and he was changed.

Now, our plan to wait it out in the front yard won't always work. Don't go making a formula out of this example, because being committed to real relationships with others isn't about finding an adultery cure-all! The point is, friends in covenant relationship are committed to one another, no matter what. Plenty of Christian friends would abandon a buddy who fell into sin. But what hope does someone have of repenting if we leave them all alone? We can't speak the truth in love if we haven't loved first. And we love first by being kind to others in practical ways, regardless of whether they deserve it.

In other words, covenant means you stand beside someone even when they fail miserably. *Especially* when they fail miserably. But you don't leave them there. Real love pleads with lost souls and stumbling Christians, "Don't go over this cliff!" You help them find their way back to the truth. You lead them home with love.

Let me ask you a question: Has there ever been a time when you've really needed a friend? Maybe something happened to you, someone in your family was seriously injured, or someone cheated on you. Maybe someone hurt you and then others gossiped about you. Maybe the situation even deteriorated to the point that you didn't want to show your face in public because you were so embarrassed. In that moment, what you probably needed was some encouragement. Even a simple acknowledgment of your pain would have sufficed, but all you got was a cheap, "I'll pray for you," and you knew they didn't mean it. I think we've all been there.

Check out what Romans 2:1–4 has to say about this type of situation. *The Message* puts it this way:

> Those people are on a dark spiral downward. But if you think that leaves you on the high ground where you can point your finger at others, think again. Every time you criticize someone, you condemn yourself. It takes one to know one. Judgmental criticism of others is a well-known way of escaping detection in your own crimes and misdemeanors. But God isn't so easily diverted. He sees right through all such smoke screens and holds you to what *you've* done.
>
> You didn't think, did you, that just by pointing your finger at others you would distract God from seeing all your misdoings and from coming down on you hard? Or did you think that because he's such a nice God, he'd let you off the hook? Better think this one through from the beginning. God is kind, but he's not soft. In kindness he takes us firmly by the hand and leads us into a radical life-change.

Did you catch that last statement? This is how God works with us. He is patient with us, when He has every right to punish us for our sin. He shows us kindness. Whether it's the way someone may have treated you in the past or an opportunity you currently have to respond to others in a different way than you have been treated before, it's the kindness of God that leads to repentance. The way you say what you say—with kindness—is equally as important as what you say.

Once I was at the mall when I noticed a man I was angry with because he had cheated on his wife and stolen some of her money. As soon as he saw me, he immediately hid behind a partition. My first thought was, *Look at him. He's so convicted, he can't even get close to me.*

The Holy Spirit whispered, *No, he's hiding because you don't love him.*

So I went up to him and said, "Hey, what's going on? I saw you hiding."

He said, "I'm not hiding!"

I just kept at him. "Yeah, when we saw each other, you immediately hid behind this partition." He denied it three times before I said, "I know why you're hiding. You're hiding because you know I don't love you right now. And for that, I'm sorry." We prayed together, and soon after that, he started coming back around the church and its people. It's the kindness of God that leads to repentance. It really does.

Sometimes being a friend in practical ways means you have a transparent conversation with them, but not always. Sometimes you need to talk, but sometimes, and maybe even more often, you just need to hang out, go to a game, or watch Netflix. Regardless of how you spend your time, do whatever you do in a kind way and say whatever you say with kindness.

Sometimes Real Love Hurts

Sometimes real love requires you to wade into someone else's pain. Sometimes the pain is deep, and you may not know how to respond or what to do. People live and then they die. There's a stat on that. I think it's 100 percent of the people who are born will also die. And here you've spent all this time learning to love someone and then their spouse or child checks out early—a life cut short. What do you do? How do you display real love in a practical way when someone is deeply grieving?

Tip of the day: honor your friend by respecting their time and privacy. It can be a balancing act. When you come alongside someone in their grief, you become privy to their thoughts and feelings, and you may get an inside scoop on their situation. But don't be the first one to put their stuff on social media, unless they've specifically asked you to. Don't be a cowboy or the first reporter on the scene. Instead, be there for them behind the scenes. Real love brings the best comfort.

Include your friend in your normal, everyday routine. Real relationships mean you are in it for the long haul, so invite your friend to do life with you. And don't force your conversations; instead, be sensitive to your friend's needs and follow their lead. I've had friends who have taken years to talk about their grief and pain, so let your friend open up if and when they are ever ready. And don't be disappointed if they never share anything.

A few years back, Jill, the wife of one of our executive pastors, went into the hospital with complications from a cancer treatment. Our staff rallied around their amazing family and went on a twenty-four-hour-a-day prayer vigil that lasted several weeks. I believe, because of that, Jill was able to have strength to attend her daughter's wedding. Sadly, the Lord chose to take Jill home a few months after that.

For those who have experienced loss, some days might always be more difficult than others. We must do our best to recognize those days—like holidays and birthdays, for example. Real love keeps in contact, even after the crisis has passed.

Conclusion

In the early days of planting New Life Church, I knew it would be a place where Michelle and I would make lifelong friends and cultivate best friends who would turn down fantastic jobs just to stay close to the friends who loved them. And that's exactly what happened.

Others packed up and moved from great jobs in other states to join New Life because they heard it was a place where they could have lasting relationships. Many people will tell you that what brought them to New Life was the music, the preaching, or the children's ministries. But if you ask them what caused them to stay, the answer is always the same—relationships. Being connected. Friends.

When you have committed to a covenant relationship with someone, you have committed to love, protect, and serve one another, even when you don't agree. It's not just about how you feel. The *issue* is not what matters most—*people* matter. It's hard to make selfish decisions when you're committed to honoring others. When you finish reading this book, my hope is that you will be a better friend to everyone you come in contact with, despite your differences.

As we learn to view relationships through the lens of real love, marriages, families, friendships, ministry relationships, and other relationships within the church find new meaning, new value, and new life! And when we relate to one another with real love instead of operating as an institution based on authority or tradition, we become an ever-expanding family, united in a healthy spirit founded on love and full of life!

Once you begin establishing these principles of relating, you'll find them spilling over into all of your relationships—whether at work or on the ball field or wherever! The principles of real love affect how you relate to everyone, which is what we'll discuss in the next chapter.

6

Welcome Home

Maybe you were born perfect, but I wasn't!

I thought I was doing a neighbor lady a favor one day. This was years before I met Michelle, and I was kind of interested in getting to know this particular pretty lady. The only problem was she had a cat, but I was willing to overlook that fact. At least for the time being.

Well, one cold morning I went outside to warm up my car, and when I cranked the engine, I heard a strange clunking sound. If you guessed that a certain cat had curled up in the engine—and didn't survive—you would be guessing correctly. But that's not the mistake I made. The mistake I made was how I broke the news to my neighbor. Since I was not certain it was her cat, I gently wrapped up the bloody mess in a towel and brought it over to her house to confirm. I knocked on her front door, and when she opened it, I was standing there holding a mangled cat. Reluctantly I said, "I'm sorry to ask, but is this your cat?" I thought it was a good idea, but it turns out I was wrong. I will put it to you this way: I am so glad I never dated that girl! She freaked out.

We all have neighbors who make bad decisions, like I did that day. And we all work with or go to church with other Christians who are, well, weird. Or, at the very least, you know other Christians who like music you don't like, who vote for candidates you can't support, or who you generally can't imagine getting along with.

In chapter 5 we talked about developing real and authentic love in our relationships, specifically our closest ones. In this chapter we're talking about how to extend some of the principles of real love to all believers. No, you can't be best friends with everyone, but you can be a friend to everyone. You can at least be friendly with everyone.

The way I like to think about it is that you are only transparent with a few, but you should be authentic with everyone. This isn't really about "levels" of relationships. This is about being the kind of person other people want to be around; the kind of person people feel safe and welcome around.

And remember, when Jesus pursues a covenant relationship with us, He does so in the *midst* of our mess. He doesn't wait until we clean up our act and *then* approach us. He doesn't wait until we share His opinions and tastes. He certainly doesn't waste His time looking for perfect people to relate to. No. Because people matter so much to Jesus, He pursues them right where they are. We have to learn to do the same thing.

The Value of a Soul

In Jesus's day, some people were complaining about the kind of company He kept. He was eating with sinners, and the religious leaders were gossiping about it. Jesus responded to them by telling this story:

> If a man has a hundred sheep and one of them gets lost, what will he do? Won't he leave the ninety-nine others in the wilderness and go to search for the one that is lost until he finds it? And when he has found it, he will joyfully carry it home on his shoulders. When he arrives, he will call together his friends and neighbors, saying, "Rejoice with me because I have found my lost sheep." In the same way, there is more joy in heaven over one lost sinner who repents and returns to God than over ninety-nine others who are righteous and haven't strayed away! (Luke 15:4–7 NLT)

This parable communicates an important principle I call "identifying the value of a soul." Jesus knew a shepherd doesn't look at a flock of sheep and say, "Ninety-nine or a hundred—same difference." No! That shepherd doesn't care for the flock as a group. He cares for each sheep individually. He believes in the value of *one*—the value of a soul. You'll never be attentive to others if you're not interested in the value of a soul, if you don't appreciate the value each person brings to the body of Christ. Despite their strange habits or unique opinions, every believer is part of God's flock. God values each of them. And that means we should too.

If you've heard a sermon on this parable from Luke 15, you might have heard a pastor explain that Jesus wants us to go out to the lost world and reach them for Jesus. That's true. But that's not really what Jesus was talking about. The lost sheep in Jesus's parable was an Israelite—one of God's chosen people—who used to be in relationship with God but, because of poor choices or life circumstances, wandered off. Understanding the value of a soul like this begins with appreciating each person's uniqueness, celebrating their differences, and maximizing their potential. It means seeing who God created them to be, regardless of their past or their mistakes. Acknowledging the value of a soul plants in us a seed of willingness to build others up, encourage others, and call the greatness out of them.

The Bible describes King David as a "man after [God's] own heart" (1 Sam. 13:14). God saw the potential in David to be king long before anyone else did, probably including David. That's because God always sees the potential in people. It's like the difference between puppies and kittens. You can always tell a puppy's potential by looking at the size of his feet. If he's a little puppy with huge feet, you know he has the potential to be a big dog. But a cat's feet won't tell you anything. Why? Because cats don't have potential! They're just cats.

Please forgive me! The only cat I like is a fighting LSU Tiger. If it makes you feel better, my little Yorkie dog looks like a cat. Maybe that is why I don't have much of a relationship with him.

My point is, we should interact with everyone based not only on who they are, but also with expectation of who they could be.

Years ago, someone reached out to be my friend, and it ended up radically changing my life forever. Michelle and I were contemplating what our next move should be. Should we plant a church in Florida or Oklahoma? Should we pastor a preexisting church rather than start one from the ground up?

It was during this season of transition that a friend of mine from Arkansas heard I was a huge Michael Jordan fan, so he invited me to go to Chicago to watch a Bulls game. I wasn't about to pass up that chance!

While we were in Chicago, this new friend began trying to convince me to move to Arkansas. My response? "No way will I *ever* move to Arkansas! No way!" I was adamant, but he insisted I do two things before giving a final no. He said I must pray about it, and I must visit the state with him. So I agreed—I prayed about it, and I visited Arkansas.

Well, it's obvious that we did move to Arkansas, and yes, it was a God idea and not just a good idea. I could talk all day long about the positive results from that decision. On a personal level, my life was changed because this one man presented me with an expectation of who I could be. He believed in me more than I believed in myself. He truly trusted that God could build a church in Arkansas through me. My confidence was shaken, and I was terrified of the prospect of starting a church with nothing. But this was exactly where God wanted me to be, and somehow my friend was clued in to that. I shudder to think what might have happened if this guy had agreed with me when I said, "No way!" to Arkansas.

Jesus Wants Everyone

When the Pharisees asked the disciples, "Why does your teacher eat with tax collectors and sinners?" (Matt. 9:11), it was clear just by the fact they asked the question that Jesus understood His mission. If He wasn't seeking out tax collectors and sinners to eat with, they wouldn't have bothered even asking the question! But what was His response? "It is not the healthy who need a doctor, but the sick. But go and learn what this means: 'I desire mercy, not sacrifice.' For I have not come to call the righteous, but sinners" (vv. 12–13). He loved everyone right where they were—all shapes and sizes, the morally bankrupt, the confused, and the doubting. And He still does.

In that same verse, Jesus hinted at how many people He wants to bring into the kingdom when He said, "For I have not come to call the righteous, but sinners." How many people are sinners? That's right! Every single person!

All of us. You. And me.

Jesus simply wants everybody in the kingdom. In 2 Peter 3:9, Peter writes, "The Lord is not slow in keeping his promise, as some understand slowness. Instead he is patient with you, not wanting *anyone* to perish, but *everyone* to come to repentance" (emphasis added). Because God wants *everyone* in His kingdom, I believe the church—my church, your church, and your small group—should never stop growing. God wants His house full because growth is His will. And people are still out there who need to know Jesus.

Is It Safe Here?

Just like the ninety-nine sheep you're turning around and leading back to the pen, the lost one you're searching for needs to know the fold they are returning to is a *safe place.* Otherwise, they won't stay long enough to experience healing, strengthening, and growth. Therefore, it is important to learn how to create a hospitable atmosphere where people can be themselves.

During our church membership class, we make a point using a story about a fictitious guy named Joe. We tell the attendees that Joe used to be in a church, but over a period of time he fell away. One group of Christians would look at Joe's condition and say, "Joe was never saved; if he was saved he could never fall away." These are the people who believe you can never lose your salvation. Another group would disagree, saying, "No, Joe did love God, but now he is lost." There are others who believe you can be saved and then lost again. Many churches have divided over issues just like this, and their doctrinal disagreement is the only thing they recognize. During the membership class, we describe this disagreement with such emotion that people sit and wait for our answer to see if they can join our church. (By the way, there is room in our church for both groups!)

We then explain the intrinsic problem with both of these positions—the focus is not on the *person*, Joe. We tell the attendees, "It doesn't matter *why* you think Joe is messed up. Let's just call him and see how we can show him love." A person who understands Joe has value will make the call. They believe Joe can be rescued and will work to create a safe place where he can grow and heal.

Scandalous Hospitality

Michelle and I love hosting people in our home. It's one of our favorite things to do. And Michelle really loves it when I bring people home unannounced, especially on laundry days! Okay, not exactly. But it is true that we enjoy getting to know people. And yes, I have learned over the years to give her advance notice if I'm bringing someone by the house (more than simply calling her as I'm pulling in the driveway!).

If you were asked who would be on your bucket list of people to hang out with for a few hours, who would it be? For me, it would be Jack Nicklaus, Michael Jordan, and Bill Gates. It used to be Dr. Billy Graham, but fortunately God answered my prayers on that one, and I was able to spend some time with him a few years back. But what about the *other* end of your list? Who are the people you would *least* prefer to hang out with? What about people who aren't anywhere *near* your circle? Would you invite someone from a completely different political viewpoint or theological position into your home? How about an atheist or agnostic?

Showing hospitality to people who don't line up with our personal views or interests can be complicated and difficult. When we start focusing on the difficulties, we miss the whole point. Jesus, instead, gave us a radical command regarding hospitality. In His day, dinner parties weren't just about having a good time. They were about impressing neighbors, making business connections, and getting ahead in the social world. Jesus told His disciples not to play those games. "When you put on a luncheon or a banquet . . . don't invite your friends, brothers, relatives, and rich neighbors." Well, why not? "For they will invite you back, and that will be your only reward." Then Jesus scandalously redefined the guest list. "Instead," He said, "invite the poor, the crippled, the lame, and the blind. Then at the resurrection of the righteous, God will reward you for inviting those who could not repay you" (Luke 14:12–14 NLT). Wow! Eternal reward is a pretty big payoff for inviting a few people to dinner.

The point Jesus was making is that hospitality isn't about us. When we truly value a soul, we recognize that it's not their job to make us feel affirmed and validated. It's our job to take care of them, to make them feel welcome. Romans 12:13 challenges us to "practice hospitality." The Greek word for "hospitality" in that verse is *philoxenia*, which literally means "love to strangers." In fact, every time the word *hospitality* is used in the New Testament, it is referencing kindness to strangers. In other words, our job as believers is not just to feel happy and comfortable and content around our best friends. Or even people most like us. Our job is to create an environment where all believers feel welcome. And we have to get this right. Because if we can't get this right with other believers, then we'll never get it right when it comes time to show hospitality to a lost and sinful world.

To practice New Testament hospitality, we must be willing to reach out to people who are beyond our comfort zone. We must be courageous enough to include those with whom we are only vaguely familiar, even total strangers. We must constantly make an effort to form new friendships. And when we practice hospitality, it is important to note that *warmth is key*.

Warmth

The concept of warmth is essentially creating a life-giving atmosphere where people don't want to leave because they feel accepted, healed, and blessed. This simple concept is vital to building an environment where people truly feel welcome. Kudos to Publius in Acts 28:7 for setting the example:

> There was an estate nearby that belonged to Publius, the chief official of the island. He welcomed us to his home and showed us generous hospitality for three days.

Publius must have been a master at hospitality, since nobody wanted to leave his house! A friend of mine used to have people over often, but on one particular evening, the group wouldn't leave. He dropped a few hints, but they stayed. He finally called his wife into their bedroom to strategize. Their conversation went something like this: "I don't know what to do! I've tried everything. I was polite. I dropped hints. I was direct. I turned up the heat. What's wrong with them? They won't leave!" The couple then returned to the living room to find their guests with shocked faces—they had been listening to the whole conversation as it was transmitted on a baby monitor!

When was the last time you invited people over for dinner and they stayed for *three days*? Not me! I enjoy entertaining visitors, but when it's my bedtime, I go to bed. I just pray they're not still hanging around the next morning! I like this verse:

Do not forget to show hospitality to strangers, for by so doing some people have shown hospitality to angels without knowing it. (Heb. 13:2)

Since there were no planes, trains, or automobiles back when the writer of Hebrews penned this verse, travelers would be gone for days or even weeks. Travel would have been very expensive if they had had to rely on covering the cost of inns and restaurants (if any existed where they were going), so it was common for people to open their homes to travelers. Some payment or gift was offered in exchange for the hospitality, but not full compensation, not like staying in a hotel. Compared to Bible times, we have it easy!

Here are some practical tips that will help you develop hospitality and build warmth when you're hosting. Remember, the temperature of the room is affected by how you connect with the people in it. You don't have to neglect your friends, but before you even enter the room, pray and ask the Lord to show you who He wants you to connect with the most. People notice when you don't spend adequate time with them. It's nearly impossible in a large crowd; it's essential when you're in a more intimate setting.

Remember to practice the same level of warmth and hospitality wherever you are, regardless of the setting. Don't let who you are when you're around your family be totally different from who you are when you're around others. That's not hospitable behavior; that's being a hypocrite. One of my closest friends, Neil, came on staff with us several years ago, and I'm so glad he did. He had dinner with us on a Saturday night, then visited the church the next day. He said as soon as he walked into the foyer of the church, he felt the same way he did in my living room. I can't take credit—that's Michelle's strength. I always want to have a party to have fun with everyone, while she wants to make sure they feel at home, welcome, and accepted. Everybody needs that.

Get to Know People

If you're just not a natural at hospitality, where do you start? Begin by learning how to get to know other people, including people who are different from you. Start conversations. Sometimes you have to ask questions to get real conversations going. Try asking "get-to-know-you" questions, such as "Where were you born?" "How long have you been married?" "What was the happiest day since you've been married?" If you don't know where to start when you meet someone, learn something about who they are or what kinds of things they're interested in.

However, listening attentively to their answers does *not* mean quietly sitting by while a person tells explicit details about every aspect of their life. A well-placed question can change a directionless conversation into one of purpose, because it requires the person to communicate on a different level. For example, if someone is frustrated with their job or wishes they made more money or had greater influence, I might ask them, "Have you considered that you might be keeping score the wrong way?"

One time I was on an airplane, writing a sermon about love. The woman sitting beside me asked, "What do you do for a living?" I hesitated before I said, "I'm a pastor of a church."

"A *what*?" she asked.

I answered again, "A pastor of a church. I'm a preacher."

She did just about everything but roll her eyes. I tried to keep the conversation going, but it didn't go well, so I went back to writing the sermon. When I was finished, I said, "Listen, I could tell you were a little irritated before when I said I was a pastor. I get it. Pastors are often bad examples, and we get spicy when we shouldn't. We can have bad attitudes, and we can be the worst! But could you help me? I'm going to be ministering to a lot of people who hate Christianity. Can you read this and tell me where I'm wrong?"

By the time she finished reading it, you could tell she was a little rattled. She never cried, but she was choked up, for sure. She handed it back and simply said, "That was refreshing."

"What do you mean?" I asked.

"Well, it was just a good angle," she said. I could tell she was moved. Was it because I wrote it well? I don't think so. I think it was because I honored her by respecting her opinion in the moment. That's a well-placed question.

It doesn't always work out like that, though. Once a man sitting next to me asked what I did for a living. I told him I was a pastor, and he said, "That's what I thought." Well, I asked him to read the sermon I was working on, and after he finished it, he said, "I read your sermon, and you seem like a real weak person to me."

"What do you mean?" I asked.

Without hesitation, he responded, "You are not worth the explanation." He was a blast!

Another kind of question I like to ask to get to know someone often leads to an optimistic answer, especially if I'm in a conversation with someone who struggles with pessimism or negativity. I ask questions that cause people to look on the positive side of issues, give them a nudge toward hopefulness. For example, "Do you think God could forgive you for what you have done?" "Do you think God could put your marriage back together?" "What would you like to see God do in your life?"

Because most people tend toward negative thinking, people generally need something positive to think about, some encouragement. For example, the weather person tells us there is a 30 percent chance of rain. But isn't that also a 70 percent chance of sunshine? We open up a loaf of bread and call it the "end." Isn't that the beginning? We ask someone for directions to our destination. They commonly say, "Go to the second red light and take a left, etc." I always ask, "What if the light is green?"

Sometimes the perfectly designed question evokes an answer that reveals hurt, regret, or excuses about why a person has not achieved what God has placed on their heart. For instance, one time I was meeting with a man who was burning the candle at both ends to grow his business. He was drinking too much coffee to stay awake during the day and too much booze to sleep at night. He was struggling to find rest. I asked him, "What are you doing that's going to matter in eternity?" To someone who feels trapped, I might ask, "If there were no barriers in front of you, what would God want you to do?" They begin to dream again, sensing I believe something better is possible for them. Let's look at Romans 12:9–13 together:

> Love must be sincere. Hate what is evil; cling to what is good. Be devoted to one another in love. Honor one another above yourselves. Never be lacking in zeal, but keep your spiritual fervor, serving the Lord. Be joyful in hope, patient in affliction, faithful in prayer. Share with the Lord's people who are in need. Practice hospitality.

This passage is clear. We must love a person sincerely before we challenge things about them that don't reflect God's character. And get this: the other person—not you—decides if your love is sincere. If they don't feel sincere love from you, then you are not loving them sincerely. This verse relates to every one of us in everyday life, because if you don't love me, I'm not going to listen to you. However, if you love me, you can correct or rebuke me all day long. Christians, even those in leadership, get this wrong all the time. We must remember: sincere love comes first!

Ask Simple Questions

When Jesus was thirsty and stopped for a drink of water from the Samaritan woman, He asked a simple and ordinary question: "Will you give me a drink?" This seemingly straightforward question started a dialogue that ultimately caused her to recognize Him as Christ. But could Jesus have begun this conversation by telling her what He already knew—that she had five husbands and was living in adultery? Maybe, but I believe she would have become defensive and not at all open to hearing Him. He started with a simple question and was patient in allowing her to question Him. As a result, she was able to receive "living water" from the true source.

I give similar advice to single people wanting to start up a conversation with someone they may be interested in dating. I suggest they go to the coffee shop and just ask the person they're interested in, "Hey, you want a scone?" It's a simple question. I know a guy who took my advice. He married the girl six months later! I told him he should call his first child either "scone" or "Rick."

Pay Attention

A good conversation is when you're purposely doing the majority of the listening. When you choose to do this, you're also choosing to honor the other person, because you're demonstrating that life isn't all about *you*. In counseling situations, most of the time I will get a couple to talk about themselves, and by the end of the session, they think I'm a genius. I didn't say much—I didn't have to!

People can tell if you are truly listening to them. When I'm in a conversation, I look at the person I'm talking to. If somebody else pats me on the back or tries to cut in, I choose to pay attention to the person with whom I am already engaged in conversation. I'm not going to get interrupted. When you practice being attentive to others (and it does take practice), it is important not to allow other people to distract you from the person God has placed in front of you. I'm not saying it's okay to be rude and ignore the new person who approaches you—just keep going with the conversation that's in front of you.

The Bible contains many examples of Jesus being *attentive to the one*. When He was walking through a huge crowd, a sick lady reached out and touched His robe. He was attentive to her (see Luke 8:43–48). When Nathanael asked Jesus how He knew him, Jesus responded, "I saw you while you were still under the fig tree" (John 1:48). He noticed him. On the cross, Jesus told John to take care of His mother (see John 19:26–27). He paid attention to the needs of others.

The ability to listen well is not innate. We may be born with two ears and one mouth, but that does not mean we are natural listeners. Communication is a process, and sometimes, even while we're actively listening, stuff just gets lost in translation. Take my brother, Randy, for instance. I remember one time when we were kids and Dad was getting ready to go on a business trip to Miami. Randy asked him, "Why are you going to your ammi?"

"I'm not going to your ammi," Dad responded, "I'm going to Miami!"

Confused, Randy shot back, "That's what I *said*! You're going to *your ammi*!"

Sometimes, no matter how hard we try, we think we understand what is being said, but we just don't get it. The truth is, many of us don't try hard to understand. We are not born with a desire to listen to others talk while we remain silent and attentive. If any proof is ever needed to support this point, I tell my church to peek inside the nursery. Scratching, fighting, or some sort of destructive behavior can probably be witnessed due to the selfish nature of our youngest members. They often don't care much for listening. It is a trait that must be developed with as much intention and discipline as a competitive weight lifter.

The apostle James writes that a controlled tongue is the sign of a mature person.

> My dear brothers and sisters, take note of this: Everyone should be quick to listen, slow to speak and slow to become angry. (James 1:19)

And James 3:2 says,

> We all stumble in many ways. Anyone who is never at fault in what they say is perfect, able to keep their whole body in check.

Learning how to listen closely to others has been a real challenge for me, so I know if I can do it, you can too. Make a commitment to be an attentive listener and, therefore, a good friend. A cost is often associated with listening that we don't take into account until we're in the middle of what may feel like a draining conversation. The other person needs a listening ear, and maybe they haven't had one in a long time. In that moment, you need to take a backseat. Don't talk about yourself, and don't advance your agenda.

When you're listening, you're practicing selflessness at the same time. Luke 6:38 says, "Give and it shall be given to you . . . pressed down, shaken together and running over." This applies to everything you are able to give, including your time and attention. On occasion, you may not even be able to stick to your schedule, because often it seems like someone needs a listening ear when it's not convenient for you. Take on the inconvenience! This has happened to me more times than I can count, and I just can't worry about my schedule anymore. I know that somehow God will redeem the time, because He always has. It just seems like God always returns time to me that I sacrifice for someone else.

Just listen. You can't fulfill a need or help solve a problem if you don't listen to what it is. Sometimes people just need to vent. Just listen. And sometimes we need to recognize a correction we need to make within ourselves. Just listen. Let me summarize with this: God gave us two ears. Use them!

Give Honor

A few years ago, I took my family to visit the Tomb of the Unknown Soldier at Arlington National Cemetery, just outside of Washington, DC, where we watched the changing of the guard. If you've ever seen the changing of the guard or a funeral with full military honors, it is truly an experience you won't soon forget.

Not just anyone can guard the tomb. In fact, even though tomb guards are volunteers, those who serve follow strict guidelines. They must have an unblemished military record, be in superb physical condition, and complete an extensive application process that includes reciting verbatim from memory a seven-page history of Arlington National Cemetery. They then practice a series of steps, pauses, and turns with precision before being chosen to guard the tomb.

I learned a lot about honor that day. One thing in particular happened just as a guard began his duty. A bumblebee started flying around his head. I pointed out the bee to my kids, and we started taking bets on how long it would take the guard to swat the bee away. But he stood perfectly still. The bumblebee landed on the guard's nose, but he stood perfectly still. Eventually, the bumblebee flew off. We were impressed! In fact, we were laughing about it as quietly as we could. (Okay, Michelle may have gotten on me about my behavior.)

But soon, we were even more impressed. Over the next few minutes, the guard's nose started turning red. Eventually it swelled up to the size of a Ping-Pong ball! He looked like Rudolph! But he never flinched. He never moved an inch. He never scowled at me for laughing, either. Nope. That guard took a bee sting in honor of a soldier whose name he will never know.

My pastor, Brother Larry Stockstill, recently spoke at our church about how honor is one of the most critical principles in God's kingdom. Honor is the gravity of the kingdom of God. Gravity is always working, but you don't see it. If gravity could be turned off like a light switch, everything in the room would start floating, including the people in it. Things and people would collide into one another, and all kinds of chaos would ensue. But if you turned the switch back on, everything would fall back into place, and we would again have a semblance of order. Honor is like a switch that we choose to turn off and on again, but God desires that we keep it on all the time. And it is God's desire that we honor everybody, starting with honoring Him as the Creator of all things. In fact, to worship God is simply to honor Him. When we honor Him, He gets close to us. We honor God when we tithe, and we honor Him when we give Him the first part of our day.

First Peter 2:17 says, "Show proper respect to everyone, love the family of believers, fear God, honor the emperor." The apostle Peter wrote this when Nero, the worst Caesar in history, was emperor of Rome. Nero used to roll Christians in pitch, then set them on fire to give light to his gardens, while he rode through them naked, on his horse, with his gay lover by his side. How in the world could Peter tell people to "honor the emperor"? Sometimes we ask the same question about our own elected officials, regardless of which party they represent. Brother Larry defined honor as "looking past the person to the position that he or she represents." Peter asks us to honor the position of emperor—or president, in our case—even if the person who holds the office doesn't deserve it. We should look past the individual who is in the office to honor the office they occupy.

Honor is about how we treat people. All people are made in God's image. That's the office they occupy. That means whether we agree with them or even like them, we can look past the person and show them the honor they deserve as someone made in God's image. Sometimes showing them honor is the only way they will live up to their calling to bear God's image.

Conclusion

When we begin to understand that Jesus pursues us in the midst of our mess, the humility of that thought challenges us to pursue others in the same way—in the midst of *their* mess. And the way we do that can make it or break it for the other person. When we create an environment where people feel warm, accepted, and welcome, they will invariably feel safe to engage with us and others in meaningful ways. When we begin to value individuals—even in their mess—the way Jesus does, we will go out of our way to demonstrate His love to them. The way we respond potentially gives them less mess to sift through, and they may even begin to see that God does love them. When we do all this, we are showing real love in a world that needs it.

7

Vegas, Baby!

One New Year's Eve, my family and I traveled to Las Vegas to ring in the new year. Unfortunately, people from Westboro Baptist Church made an appearance too. A group of them was standing on a street corner, yelling at everybody. They were sharing their version of the "Good News": Turn or burn. God hates you.

At one point one of them screamed to a man in the crowd, "Your wife is a whore!" He then screamed that to the crowd I was standing in. I was about to break his face, but then I remembered, *I can't fight very well*. I've been in only one fight my whole life, and I came in third place. Anyway, these angry "Christians" were yelling that our wives weren't pure, and people were laughing at them, but I was humiliated. Christianity has certainly seen better times. The problem was, these street evangelists were speaking *some* truth. But they were doing it in the wrong place and definitely in the wrong way. Trust me, they were not effective!

On the other side of the street, opposite the Westboro Baptists, was a young guy holding a sign that read "John 3:16" and "Jesus loves you!" He also had a huge smile on his face. He was just standing there quietly. I went over and hugged the guy and thanked him for what he was doing. He provided a stark contrast to the openly hateful "Christians" just across the street. I was so shocked by their behavior. It was truly mind-boggling how poorly they treated people. It's pretty obvious to everyone that this isn't the most effective way to engage the world with the truth of the gospel. Even if people are lost and in danger of spending eternity in hell, screaming at strangers in the street is an epic fail.

Obviously the angry protesters from Westboro Baptist Church do not speak for all Christians. Most Christians would quickly distance themselves from their hateful messages. The problem is, the rest of the world doesn't always make that distinction. The lost world outside the church often lumps us all in together—you and me and Westboro Baptist. And, if we're honest, we have to see why. We might not be *that* angry and *that* judgmental. But it is true that we believers, who have been given two simple commandments—love God with all your heart, soul, mind, and strength; and love your neighbor as yourself—do sometimes get judgmental, mean-spirited, cruel, and vicious even, toward others. Why? Christians who have lost concern for others and become issues-driven tend to develop a messiah complex. They think they can convict people of their sin and save us all from hell with their good deeds. I'm convinced that some of those who lose their cool like that are simply demonstrating that they feel threatened.

It's funny—no, really, it's sad. The spirit of the Pharisees lives on, even at our church where we try hard to teach people not to be judgmental. Michelle has always been a huge Céline Dion fan, so for her fortieth birthday, I took her to see the singer in concert in Las Vegas. When we returned from that vacation, two families left our church simply because we went to Vegas. Sure, a lot of people go to Vegas to do the wrong things, but I took my wife there to see Céline Dion. Some people just assume the worst. I think it's because they feel threatened.

But why do they feel threatened? If that's you, why do you feel threatened? It's really no wonder. Television news is designed to keep people angry and fearful. Politicians prey on our insecurities. They secure votes by convincing us to assume the worst of people—to believe everyone's out to limit our freedom or steal our cars. Many of us worry we will lose our freedom to worship and get sent to prison or otherwise be persecuted for our faith. As a result, many people—even Christians—live every day of their lives afraid of something, and they're eager to know who their enemy is so they know who to be afraid of!

By the way, I'm not opposed to the idea that we are living in the end of the end-times, the beginning of persecution. It sure feels like we are! Explore how Jesus described the events that will lead up to the end-times:

> Take heed that no one deceives you. For many will come in
> My name, saying, "I am the Christ," and will deceive many.
> And you will hear of wars and rumors of wars. See that

you are not troubled; for all these things must come to pass, but the end is not yet. For nation will rise against nation, and kingdom against kingdom. And there will be famines, pestilences, and earthquakes in various places. All these are the beginning of sorrows. (Matt. 24:4–8 NKJV)

And when people consistently reject Christ, the following results:

Then they will deliver you up to tribulation and kill you, and you will be hated by all nations for My name's sake. And then many will be offended, will betray one another, and will hate one another. Then many false prophets will rise up and deceive many. And because lawlessness will abound, the love of many will grow cold. But he who endures to the end shall be saved. And this gospel of the kingdom will be preached in all the world as a witness to all the nations, and then the end will come. (vv. 9–14 NKJV)

We could unpack a ton in these passages, but the main point I want to highlight is in verse 12: "Because lawlessness will abound, the love of many will grow cold." That's the worst-case scenario. Christians suffering opposition and persecution is not the worst-case scenario. What's worse is that Christians will lose hope in light of all these things. Instead of reaching out in love, their love will grow cold.

But that ominous warning doesn't include *you*. Growing cold isn't who you are. Pressing into the heart of God is who you are, standing firm in your faith in Him is who you are, and growing in boldness to share His love for your neighbors in an environment where they feel loved and accepted right where they are—*that* is who you are. Remember how God met you and loved you exactly where you were on that day when you said yes to Him? And do you see how He loved you too much to leave you there? He still feels that way—about you *and* your neighbor!

Who Is My Neighbor?

Many of us, as Christians, feel like our values are being attacked by the broader culture around us. When we feel attacked, two natural responses are fight or flight. We are tempted to either fight the people who are caught up in or leading the culture shift or run away from the culture altogether. But neither of those options is what God has in mind for us. God has a third option for those who want to walk in real love in an angry world.

Remember that Jesus summarized the entire law in two commandments—love God with all your heart and love your neighbor as yourself. Well, we know that. And because we know that, we like to try to limit the number of people who fall into the category of "neighbor." If we're honest, each of us has a list of people we can't imagine would qualify as our neighbor. The list is different for everyone. Surely God doesn't expect us to love *those people*. If we can convince ourselves that "those people" are our enemies, and not our neighbors, then maybe God doesn't expect us to love them.

When we start thinking this way—and let's be honest, we all do this at times—we're working a very old strategy. An expert in the law once approached Jesus to test Him in front of a crowd. He was trying to trip Jesus up. He asked Him, "What must I do to inherit eternal life?" Jesus answered his question with a question. Jesus liked to do that. Jesus asked the man, essentially, "How would you answer that question?"

The guy did pretty well. In fact, he answered with Jesus's familiar summary of the law: "'Love the Lord your God with all your heart and with all your soul and with all your strength and with all your mind,' and 'Love your neighbor as yourself'" (Luke 10:25–27).

Jesus said, "Good job, man. Now just go do it." That's my translation.

But the expert in the law couldn't leave it at that. He asked a follow-up question designed to justify himself. "And who is my neighbor?" he asked (Luke 10:29). The question in his mind, the one he didn't ask but wanted the answer to, was, *And just how many people do I have to love as a neighbor? Give me the smallest number possible.*

Jesus didn't really answer that question directly either. Instead, He told a story about a man, an Israelite, who was traveling from Jerusalem to Jericho. Along the way, he was attacked by bandits who beat him up and left him for dead. First, a priest walked by him. But instead of helping him out, the priest crossed the street and passed him by. Next, a Levite walked by. This was a religious leader. He did the same thing—walked past him like he wasn't even there. Next came a Samaritan. The Israelites hated the Samaritans. Samaritans felt the same way about Israelites. It doesn't really matter why. What matters is that, as far as the people listening to this story were concerned, a Samaritan was the last person who would stop to help an Israelite who was in trouble. But boy did he help. He picked the guy up, had him cared for, and paid his bill.

When Jesus finished telling His story, He asked the expert in the law, "Which of these three do you think was a neighbor to the man who fell into the hands of robbers?" (Luke 10:36).

The answer, of course, is the Samaritan—the one who met the hurting man in his need.

Who Is My Enemy?

We're tempted to keep the neighbor category small, and we tend to think of people who disagree with us politically or morally—basically that big group we call "the culture" or "the world"—as our enemies. That doesn't really help us out a whole lot, because one of Jesus's upside-down teachings is that we aren't supposed to treat enemies any differently than we treat neighbors.

Jesus challenged the conventional wisdom of the day. He said (my paraphrase), "Some of you have a saying that goes like this: 'Love your neighbor and hate your enemy.'" Then He said, in effect, "If you follow Me, that's not how we roll." Finally, He said, "But I tell you, love your enemies and pray for those who persecute you, that you may be children of your Father in heaven." Why? Because God does the same thing. "He causes his sun to rise on the evil and the good, and sends rain on the righteous and the unrighteous" (Matt. 5:44–45).

In other words, God commands us to love *everyone*—not just our neighbors. We are even to love our enemies. *Everyone*. When the world opposes us or even persecutes us, we are supposed to respond with love. Mercy. Compassion.

We don't stand for Jesus in an angry world by holding signs and shouting slogans. We don't do it through angry tweets or Facebook posts in all caps. We do it by choosing—there's covenant again—to walk in relationship with nonbelievers, as well as those closest to us and other believers.

Seasoned with Grace . . . and Salt

The big picture is that we have a job to do. We are called to demonstrate God's love to the world by living in a true community of believers that extends its love to the lost world. God has given us clear instructions about how we are supposed to live out the truth in the culture around us. He says, "You are the salt of the earth" (Matt. 5:13), and "You are the light of the world" (v. 14).

As salt, we are called to bring tasteful flavor to our culture. Scrambled eggs are good, but if you apply salt too early while cooking, the eggs won't be soft. They'll become hard, kind of rubbery. So is screaming at the culture tasteful? No, that's rude, and it has the same effect as salt applied too soon to scrambled eggs. It will cause people's hearts to harden. Colossians 4:6 says a similar thing a different way. "Let your conversation be always full of grace, seasoned with salt, so that you may know how to answer everyone." The apostle Paul wrote these words. He spent his entire ministry reaching nonbelievers. He knew that to be effective he had to season his message with the salt of grace.

We are also called to shine our light for the world to see what direction to take. Jesus says, "Let your light shine before others, that they may see your good deeds and glorify your Father in heaven" (Matt. 5:16). We are light when we demonstrate in our lives the work of the cross through our good deeds. If we miss the second half of Matthew 5:16 (the good works part) and simply shine a beacon of raw truth directly in people's faces, we do nothing but blind them further.

Maintain Innocence

If your childhood was like mine, then you've probably heard a pastor say you should "flee even the appearance of evil." This is the only real advice some people get about living in a godly way. Or maybe they quote 2 Corinthians 6:17: "Come out from them and be separate, says the Lord. Touch no unclean thing, and I will receive you." It's all about staying pure. Being in the world and not of it. All that is important.

But there's more to it than that. We also have to maintain a spirit of innocence, and that means more than just avoiding sin. Maintaining a spirit of innocence keeps your internal compass pointing to Jesus while you connect with those around you, regardless of whether or not they know Him. Innocence means not just choosing *not to* think about or participate in evil thoughts or actions yourself. That's the obvious part. But maintaining innocence also means choosing to believe the best about other people, to view others the way you want to be seen. Innocence sounds like this: "I choose to see this person the way I want Jesus to see me."

In Romans 16:19, Paul writes, "Everyone has heard about your obedience, so I rejoice because of you; but I want you to be wise about what is good, and innocent about what is evil." When you maintain a spirit of innocence, you begin living without an agenda. It means refusing to be defined and motivated by political positions, social issues, or even our own personal goals. And it means refusing to define other people by those things.

But how does innocence help us demonstrate real love? When Jesus was hanging on the cross, one of the last things He said was, "Father, forgive them, for they do not know what they are doing" (Luke 23:34). What? They don't *know* what they're doing? Come on, Jesus! You knew *they knew* they were murdering an innocent man! A Roman centurion even stood right in front of the cross and said Jesus was truly the Son of God (see Matt. 27:54; Mark 15:39). They not only knew they were murdering an innocent man, but they even knew who He was!

The story of the feeding of the five thousand also contains a demonstration of operating out of a spirit of innocence. Jesus didn't argue with the disciples when they complained they didn't have any food to share. He didn't raise His voice or resort to anger or assert His authority over the situation. He didn't have to prove anything; He was fully confident in His identity. He simply told the disciples to find out what food they had, then He directed them to organize the people into groups. He never challenged the disciples directly, and He didn't waste His time trying to explain why He was doing what He was doing. He simply demonstrated the enormity of His provision in their midst.

Jesus knows the full truth about everybody, but He chooses to see past that to our potential—if we give Him space to move into our lives—even though we don't deserve it. When we choose to believe the best about others and speak the best about others—even if we think they don't deserve it—we're choosing to live like Jesus lived. We're choosing to see the potential in them rather than the mistakes they've made.

Remember, Jesus stopped at the well to ask for a drink of water from a woman with a poor reputation, and His disciples wondered what in the world He was doing when they showed up with lunch (although they were afraid to say anything out loud). Though He knew the truth about her past, He knew her potential—He saw what could be—and called it out. The way Jesus engaged in conversation with this woman allowed her to own her past without feeling condemned because of it.

Check out how she responded in John 4:28–29: "Then, leaving her water jar, the woman went back to the town and said to the people, 'Come, see a man who told me everything I ever did. Could this be the Messiah?'" Do people in the culture around you respond the same way after they've had an encounter with you? Is it even possible? I believe so. But if we want to reach broken people, we have to deny ourselves. Bringing the broken to Him requires daily self-denial and obedience to the leading of the Holy Spirit, meaning you better be prayed up before you try it!

Too many Christians do this all wrong. One church I was part of tried to reach out to the lost through small groups. The first week, the group would gather for edification. The second week, we invited lost people to join us. However, we didn't have any idea how to treat lost people. Some of us prayed in tongues. Some started doing spiritual warfare—facing north, south, east, and west and praying against the powers of evil in each of those directions. A friend of mine came with me that night, and I was humiliated. He was freaked out. After he put up with us for a little while, he asked me to get his coat. When I gave it to him, he literally jumped a fence and ran away!

Our hearts may have been in the right place, but people couldn't stand to be around us.

A better approach came to me a little while later. One of my neighbors wasn't a Christian and was living with his girlfriend at the time. Michelle and I invited them over for dinner. We didn't have any kind of religious agenda. I think I blessed the meal, but I did it quickly. Then we just had a great night. We played cards and laughed. As they were leaving at the end of the night, the man said, "We had a great time. We'd love to have you come to our home sometime."

Friends, we have to get this right. We have to develop relationships with the lost so these people who need Jesus can't wait to be around us.

A year and a half later, I officiated at the wedding when my neighbor married that girl he was living with. It all started with dinner.

Conclusion

When there's a shift of values in a culture, people respond in different ways. If we choose to feel threatened, we can become mean-spirited, issues-driven people. But if we continue to remain in the presence of the Father, He will give us His heart of compassion. Remember what I said in chapter 3 about daily prayer? It's doubly true when we're seeking to live in love among nonbelievers. They may not know how to demonstrate real love, but they will know it when they see it.

As we seek the Father's will and His way in all our responses, we will naturally want to go where He would go, speak how He would speak, and do what He would do. This is how we bring God's love for our neighbors to our neighbors. Sometimes your neighbors will thank you for it. Other times, you just can't win. In the next chapter, I'll show you how to respond when you feel caught in the middle between the truth you know and love—Jesus—and the world He knows and loves . . . and even died for.

8

Sometimes You Just Can't Win

My family hasn't always aced everything in our relationships with one another, but one thing I am always thankful for is the laughter and joy we have shared. My mom reminded me recently that when I was four years old I sucked my thumb. She couldn't get me to stop, so she put cayenne pepper on it. That didn't stop me though; I just thought it was a new type of Cajun meal with intense flavor. Then she started making up lies, like, "If you keep sucking your thumb, you're gonna get fat. Fat, fat, fat, FAT, *FAT*!" That did it. I became very worried about getting fat. The next day I was at the store with my mom and a very pregnant lady was standing nearby. I went up to her and said, "I know what *you've* been doing!" Lord, help us all!

Joy has incredible value, but I grew up in a church where there was no laughter. No joy. No one ever laughed, unless somebody sang badly or something like that. The rules in that church were oppressive. That's why I left the church and started smoking pot with my friends. I just couldn't ever find the joy in the hearts of my fellow churchgoers that they kept woefully singing about. I think many people today still feel like I did back then. They've given up on finding joy in the church because they've never actually experienced it there.

I love it when there is real joy in a church. I love it when joy is in a home too. But just because you've invited Christ Jesus into your home doesn't mean you've received the joy He's able to give you. Martha and Mary both invited Jesus to their house, but Martha was worried and distracted—worried she wouldn't get everything right (gotta get the food right, the kids right, the house right) and distracted because Mary wasn't helping at all. Instead, Mary was sitting at Jesus's feet. Martha had enough of it and went into the living room and complained, saying, "Lord, don't you care that my sister has left me to do the work by myself?" Jesus responded, "Martha, Martha . . . you are worried and upset about many things, but few things are needed—or indeed only one. Mary has chosen what is better, and it will not be taken away from her" (Luke 10:40–42).

A man was telling me recently about how his wife has lost her joy. When he leaves work for home, he drives around the block a few times just to get the confidence to walk into the house. Home is a sad place for that man. Come to think of it, I've never met a man who has said, "I just want to marry a depressed woman who hates everybody." I believe a home should be a refuge, and joy makes it that way. But what is joy, and how do you get it? I believe, just like choosing to love one another, joy is a choice you make to view every moment you're in as a precious gift. You can choose to endure each moment with a negative attitude, or you can choose to live in joy in the moment.

In 1 Samuel 2:1, Hannah declared, "My heart rejoices in the LORD! The LORD has made me strong" (NLT). And Proverbs 31:25 says, "She is clothed with strength and dignity, and she laughs without fear of the future" (NLT). Whoa. Laughing without fear of the future is certainly timely for today. This attitude looks at the future and says yes!

It's Coming from Everywhere

Who doesn't want to live a joyful life? But sometimes, no matter how well you ace being a Christ-follower, no matter how convincingly you laugh without fear of the future, people will still hate or reject you. That's part of what it means to live in an angry world. King David lived in an angry world too. He was a brave man who conquered his enemies on countless occasions without a drop of fear. But King David went through a season when he was hated and rejected by even his own son.

One of the lowest moments in King David's life occurred when his son Absalom drew the allegiance of thousands of troops away from his father. King David and a small band of warriors were forced to flee Jerusalem to escape being slaughtered by Absalom. As King David was passing through a small village east of Jerusalem, Shimei, a man from the family of former king Saul, came running beside the group, throwing rocks and dirt at King David. He cursed the king and yelled, "Get out of here, you murderer! You scumbag!" If I had been on that horse, I might have drop-kicked Shimei across the Jordan Valley! I would have been irritated, for sure. One of King David's warriors offered to behead the fool (I mean, "the man"). But here's how King David responded:

> David then said to Abishai and all his officials, "My son, my own flesh and blood, is trying to kill me. How much more, then, this Benjamite! Leave him alone; let him curse, for the LORD has told him to. It may be that the LORD will look upon my misery and restore to me his covenant blessing instead of his curse today." (2 Sam. 16:11–12)

In this dark moment in King David's life, he just couldn't win. But how did he respond? He basically told his troops, "Leave him alone. God is using him to tell me something." What? Have you ever seen such humility, where the strongest leader around you listens intently to his accusers and accepts it as a challenge, a word from the Lord even, to restore him to God's blessing? And so Shimei continued along the way, cursing, shouting, throwing stones, and showering King David with dirt. What a day. The story ends with King David's group arriving at their destination thoroughly exhausted. I would be exhausted too if someone was pelting me with rocks all day.

You will face rejection. Sometimes you just can't win.

This is a feeling we should probably get used to. A "tolerance movement" is growing in our culture. At face value, tolerance seems like a good thing. This tolerance movement has a more aggressive definition of the word *tolerance* than any previous generation. The Bible encourages us to practice long-suffering and forbearance, showing patience and restraint toward others, while we remain firm in our convictions. But the tolerance movement doesn't just want you to be patient and show restraint. Those who support the movement want you to *agree with their position*. They don't want you to be patient in disagreement. They want everyone to agree—with them! And if you disagree, you get labeled a bigot or an idiot. No matter how gracious and hospitable you are to the world, there will always be people who think your beliefs themselves are intolerant and oppressive.

The world is not the only pushy and oppressive force we have to worry about. In response to a cultural shift away from Christian values, religious people often double down and try to take a firm and unwavering stand for the truth. The problem is, religious people are never satisfied either. John the Baptist was as serious about his faith as a person can be. He wore weird clothes and ate weird food. The religious leaders thought he was demon-possessed. Jesus ate and drank with sinners—He had a good old time. The very same religious leaders called Him a glutton and a drunkard (see Matt. 11:18–19). The point is, if you are successfully reaching out to the world, religious people will be suspicious of you.

How do you respond in this chaos? By standing firm, yes, but with contentment, peace, and joy. Joy doesn't come from what's happening around you. That is happiness. The word *happiness* comes from the root word, *happenstance*, which literally means where you happen to be standing, like you just happen to be in a happy environment. Of course you're happy! Joy is different. Joy comes from what's happening inside of you. According to the Word, "The joy of the LORD is your strength" (Neh. 8:10). Therefore, not surprisingly, the enemy will do everything he can to rob you of your joy. He absolutely despises joy. In fact, if you want to irritate the enemy even more, practice cultivating more joy in your life! Like Mary, spend time in God's presence and choose to be thankful for everything. And when accusers criticize you, don't let fear overwhelm you. Fear is not from God; it's another attack of the enemy that will also subsequently rob you of your joy.

Let's look again at the story of Shimei. We left off with him throwing rocks at King David all day. As recorded in the next three chapters of 2 Samuel, King David's troops rallied, one of his commanders killed Absalom, ending the family feud, and he mourned and returned to Jerusalem, reuniting Israel. On King David's return trip to Jerusalem, Shimei came running up to him again, only this time he apologized for his behavior. And King David, who had the right and the power to put him to death, chose to forgive him, sealing his promise with an oath.

The way I see it, instead of retreating in fear or lashing out in anger, King David let Shimei's words and rocks fly. And once the Lord restored him to his throne, King David chose not to take vengeance on Shimei. When you face accusers on one side or the other, I can't guarantee you'll roll into your kingdom on a thoroughbred, sit on your throne, and say to the subjects, "I forgive you." But I do know the Lord will have His way. Meanwhile, the Word shows us how to let the rocks fly.

Even My Own Family

In Titus 3:1–2, Paul writes about several aspects of real love in an angry world, including being "subject to rulers and authorities . . . obedient . . . ready to do whatever is good, to slander no one, to be peaceable and considerate, and always to be gentle toward everyone."

This list touches on relationships of all kinds with people in a number of different roles—from people you'll probably never meet ("rulers and authorities") to the guy who works in the cubicle next to yours. Notice Paul says our default approach in all these relationships and in every circumstance should be courtesy and kindness. Never in Scripture will you find God's approval for choosing to respond in hostility—verbally or otherwise—toward anyone.

But Paul knew people are people and that at some point you're going to have to deal with divisive and accusing believers. Paul clearly addresses how to handle this:

> But avoid foolish controversies and genealogies and arguments and quarrels about the law, because these are unprofitable and useless. Warn a divisive person once, and then warn them a second time. After that, have nothing to do with them. You may be sure that such people are warped and sinful; they are self-condemned. (Titus 3:9–11)

The Amplified Bible expands on what a divisive person looks like in this way: "such a person . . . is gratified by causing confusion among believers." Paul challenges Christians to be kind, respectful, and courteous toward *everyone*, while in the same breath warning them to get the divisive guy out of their midst. Why? Because this particular kind of person actually gets pleasure from confusing others and dividing believers. You know this person. They rant in all caps on social media. They demand you agree with their doctrinal issue or political position, and if you don't, you're not a "real" Christian. They're the co-worker whose car is covered in bumper stickers promoting all kinds of religious agendas—and you hope no one in the office finds out they're a Christian, because no one likes them. These are the Christians who make it hard for the rest of us to be Christians.

I am convinced Paul was advising Titus to respond to *everyone* in the same way, including the divisive person.

I was doing premarital counseling one day with a cute young couple, when my office door suddenly flew open. There stood a huge, muscular white man, completely blocking the doorway. Startled, we all yelped, then he yelled, "I heard that you're gonna have a n— in my daughter's wedding!" That's all he said.

At first, I had no idea who he was, until I remembered I was officiating another wedding in a few weeks. I'll call this man who barged into my office "Charlie." Charlie's daughter was getting married, and the groom's best man was African American. I also remembered Charlie was a deacon in a local church.

Well, I was a little upset that he burst in like he did, so I said, "Are you here because you're mad that we're gonna have a n— in your daughter's wedding?"

"Yeah!" he said.

"Well, I've got *great* news!" I responded. "We're not going to have a n— in your daughter's wedding, but we *are* going to have a black man."

I've never seen a man get so angry in all my life. The couple in front of me looked puzzled and shocked. It was easy to get them out of my office that day.

Because Charlie was a deacon, I called his pastor and told him what had happened. The pastor responded, "I've been a pastor here for a week, and I can't believe how racist these people are! I was thinking about preaching on that this weekend, and now I know I'm doing it!"

I remember saying, just before I hung up the phone, "Be careful now, ya hear?"

I called him back the following Monday to find out how his sermon went. He said, "You won't believe it. I thought it went great, but when I showed up at my office, they handed me a pink slip. I've been fired."

And that, my friend, is the real condition of more believers than I care to admit.

The key is to understand that boundaries are important—both boundaries of believing the story of God as it has been revealed to us in Scripture, as well as boundaries of what is and is not okay in how you treat people, which, of course, is also consistent with Scripture. So we're talking about two different types of boundaries at the same time: boundaries of what we hold as uncompromising truth and boundaries of how we choose to treat others, regardless of how they treat us. Let's tackle the first one first.

Can I at Least Have Some Guardrails?

Real love requires boundaries. You may not like the sound of boundaries, but they can save your life. Here in Arkansas, where I live, a couple of scenic highways run through the mountains that give you access to some of the most beautiful views in the state. The problem is, the roads are narrow and curvy and there's no shoulder—just a sheer drop to the bottom. Thankfully, guardrails keep you on the road and away from a sudden fall to your death.

So if you don't like the sound of boundaries, think of them as guardrails. They keep you safely on the winding, and sometimes treacherous, road of life so you can enjoy the ride.

The first set of boundaries is biblical truth. The Word contains major truths that are foundational to our faith—essential truths that Christians have believed forever. They are not the teachings of certain denominations or sects or movements, but of all believers everywhere:

- The Holy Bible is the inspired, infallible, inerrant Word of God and is totally reliable and relevant for our lives today.
- One eternal God is the Creator of all things. He exists in three Persons: God the Father, God the Son, and God the Holy Spirit. He is totally loving and completely holy.
- Sin has separated each of us from God and His purpose for our lives.
- The Lord Jesus Christ, both 100 percent God and 100 percent man, is the only One who can reconcile us to God. He was born of a virgin, lived a sinless and exemplary life, died on the cross in our place, and rose again to prove His victory and empower us for life.
- To receive forgiveness and "new birth," we must repent of our sins, believe in the Lord Jesus Christ, and submit to His will for our lives.
- To live the holy and fruitful lives God intends for us and to complete the development of Christ's character in us, we need to yield to His Word and His Spirit. Through the present ministry of the Holy Spirit and the Word of God, we are able to live godly lives.

- God has individually equipped us so that we can successfully achieve His purpose for our lives—to worship Him, fulfill our role in the church, and serve the community in which we live.
- Our eternal destination of either heaven or hell is determined by our response to the Lord Jesus Christ.
- The Lord Jesus Christ will return as He promised.
- Obedience through water baptism is instructed by the Word of God. Every new convert is to be baptized in water in the name of the Father, the Son, and the Holy Spirit.
- The Lord's Supper is a unique time of communion in the presence of God, when the elements of bread and grape juice (the body and blood of the Lord Jesus Christ) are taken in remembrance of Jesus's sacrifice on the cross.

Christians consider many other beliefs important. Things like views about the end-times; spiritual gifts, such as prophecy and healing and speaking in tongues; and styles of worship. If you ask five believers about these things, you'll probably get five different answers. For example, many people disagree about *when* Jesus is returning. Those who believe in pre-tribulation (pre-tribbers) argue Christians will be raptured before the tribulation period begins, while those who believe in mid-tribulation (mid-tribbers) think Christians will be raptured halfway through the tribulation period. Those who believe in post-tribulation (post-tribbers) argue Christians will live through the tribulation period until Jesus's return. When people ask if I'm a pre-, mid-, or post-tribber, I tell them I'm a "pan-tribber"—I believe it will all *pan out* in the end! The point is we can argue about stuff like this all day long, but the bottom line is we all agree that Jesus *is* returning. We can have discussions—or even debates—about these issues. Still, God does not permit us to be divisive over these issues.

When you find yourself being condemned by a fellow Christ-follower who doesn't agree with your theology or politics or whatever, here's my advice: don't argue with them. Proverbs 26:4 says, "Do not answer a fool according to his folly, or you yourself will be just like him." In other words, if someone comes at you ready to fight and you respond in the same tone, you'll be in a fight fast. Try this instead: ask them to tell you more about their opinion. Ask them questions. Even if you aren't all that interested, ask them to explain their view. You can then respond with something reasonable like, "I hadn't thought about it that way" or "I see where you're coming from." See what happens. Odds are you'll take the heat out of their argument, and then you can have a productive conversation.

Sometimes when you're facing a disagreement, the issue you're facing is not about disagreement. It's about how disagreement makes you feel. So it's really about discord. There are a few basic types of people you can have disagreement with, and therefore potentially have discord with: peers, those who are under your authority, those in authority over you, "those" people, and everybody else!

Disagreement and Discord with a Peer

It's okay to disagree with our peers. In fact, it's impossible to see eye to eye on everything, because each person brings a unique perspective to every situation. But when disagreement leads to discord, we need to work for resolution. A healthy thought process in this type of situation *should* be, *Hmm. I'm feeling anger (or tension or fear or irritation or whatever). Holy Spirit, show me what You're trying to teach me through this situation.* Unfortunately, people can sometimes be unwilling to own up to their part in the conflict or disagreement and let the Holy Spirit use it as a teaching moment. My advice in this type of situation is simply this: stay humble, and let God use such moments in your life to make you a better you. God can use anything and everything to change you, and the more teachable you are, the wiser you'll become and the better off you'll be.

If you feel you honestly did nothing wrong, ask yourself, *What is the 1 percent I could apologize for, even if I feel like 99 percent of this conflict is not my fault?* Then, go to that person—in person—and apologize to them for your 1 percent. A good rule of thumb is always to apologize to the other person for your 1 percent. And if the other person needs to know about something they did wrong against you, talk to them one-on-one, face-to-face. But only approach them about that thing if it is a mistake or a sin against you (see Matt. 18). People make mistakes all the time, even you, and it isn't necessary, appropriate, or enjoyable to walk around pointing out everybody else's faults. Nobody wants or needs that.

We often think that if we are mostly right, then we have the authority or ability to "win." We just need to be 51 percent right! But that's not true. We have to release all of our rights and focus on the one area where we were wrong and apologize first. Our humility softens the other person to open up about what's really going on. Instead of dealing with all the branches, we get to the root of the problem. Focus on the 1 percent you did wrong, take it on the chin, then start asking questions to get to the root of why the other person is feeling the way they are feeling.

If you can't talk to the other person in person, the next best thing is a video call or a phone call. It is never okay to "talk" through a conflict using email or text. Just remember one golden rule in regard to twenty-first-century communication in conflict: never written, always verbal, and preferably face-to-face.

Why face-to-face? Because tone of voice and body language are huge parts of communication. Those two things convey your attitude, which you want to come across as kind and accepting. In a conflict, email and texts are easily misunderstood or taken out of context. If you want to protect the relationship amid the conflict, meet in person or pick up the phone.

Disagreement and Discord with Someone *under* Your Authority

When you have a disagreement with someone who is *under* your authority, you may feel like that person isn't willing to admit they're wrong. You may feel that because you are in authority, you are probably right! In situations like this, I work to help the other person understand why I believe in the position I hold. Of course, if I'm wrong and I know it, I admit it and apologize. But if I honestly believe my way is the best way, it's my responsibility to communicate this in a reliable way, because "reliable communication permits progress" (Prov. 13:17 TLB). It's my responsibility to teach or mentor the person under my authority. If that person chooses not to listen or fall in line under that, that's on them. It's a mentoring relationship, where I am working to explain how my views differ from their views and why. It's not uncommon for someone to come back to me years later and thank me for the wisdom.

Disagreement and Discord with Someone in Authority *over* You

When you disagree with someone in authority over you, it's a good idea to remember they dig the path where water flows toward you. That means when everything works the way it's supposed to, blessing flows to you from the people in authority over you. If God put someone in leadership over you, it was not an accident. Do you believe God is the God of justice, or do you think you need to supply your own justice? It doesn't matter who the authority is. As long as I love God and serve the one over me, I am covered.

Disagreement with an authority figure can be emotional. Therefore, it's a good idea to respect those in authority over you. That way you'll have practice respecting authority when you don't agree with them about something.

Darren, the executive pastor at New Life Church, was leading a management meeting on my behalf one afternoon. Pastor Darren said something like, "There's a meeting next Tuesday at 2:00 p.m. Pastor Rick wants all staff to be there, so clear your schedules and make sure everyone on your team is there."

Someone in the meeting responded, "I was just talking to Pastor Rick, and he said the campus pastors weren't required to come."

Pastor Darren *could have* interpreted this comment as disrespectful to him personally. He could have thought the comment meant the person in the meeting was boasting that they knew more about the situation than he did. But that's not what he did. Instead, he sized up the circumstances and saw an opportunity to demonstrate honor to his lead pastor. And he responded *immediately.* "Whatever Pastor Rick says, we're going with. So campus pastors don't need to be at this meeting." Then he moved on to the next subject.

I have a real sense of urgency on my heart to overhonor, to outdo others with honor, to even surprise others with honor. People stop stressing out so much and remember they're called for community when they feel honored. Take time to honor people. Establish a culture of honor in your church, your community, and even on behalf of those the Lord has placed as governing authorities over your state and our nation.

This is especially relevant today. For example, when you see a police officer, don't avoid them. Talk to them, say something encouraging, and pray for them. Take the time to listen to the hurts of people groups who are different from you. When you do, you are honoring them and demonstrating to the culture around you how to live in an honorable way.

Disagreement and Discord with "Those" People

Then there are "those" people who seem to constantly cause discord in your life, yet you *have* to deal with them. This is common in work environments. These people are not peers necessarily. They're not in authority over you, and you're not in authority over them. Maybe they are your neighbor or a friend of a friend. Maybe you need what they offer to accomplish your work, but it seems like they work double overtime to make your life miserable in the process. This happens for a number of reasons. It could be a problem the person has with control or unforgiveness in their own life. It could be they're generally unhappy. It could be they don't know Jesus!

But who is the God of justice? Is it God or is it you? If it is you, then try to handle this on your own. Let me know how that works for you! But if it is not you, then let God be God. Check out this verse:

> This is how we know what love is: Jesus Christ laid down his life for us. And we ought to lay down our lives for our brothers and sisters. (1 John 3:16)

When in conflict with one of *those* people, ask yourself how God feels about that person. Ask yourself if you really believe what God says—that no sin is greater than another. Ask yourself if you really believe in God's resurrection power for *every* person—including that one. Continue to practice Matthew 18—choosing humility, practicing grace, and accepting second place—until the Lord either changes the other person, changes you, or delivers you from the situation.

In most of these types of relationships, it would be prideful to assume every time it is the other person who should change. Of course, in the case of abuse, it's the abuser and not the victim who needs to change. But many times, something in each person has to die—their need to be justified or right—to achieve unity. For true unity to happen, both sides have to die to themselves. Resolving discord is not about just trying to get the other person to die to themselves. There is a huge possibility that it's my opportunity to die right now. This is not easy! If it were easy, it would be called "fun," not death.

The apostle Paul tells us he has learned to become all things to all people (1 Cor. 9:22), essentially doing whatever it takes to show that unity with them and with Christ is most important. And by the way, if we agree on something Christ doesn't agree with, it doesn't count. If Jesus doesn't agree with it, we don't have unity.

I have learned over the years to treat different situations differently and different types of people differently. Sometimes you have to be bold with some people, because they may miss your subtle hints. Sometimes it's okay to "grab their face mask" to get their attention, like a football coach used to do, if that's what it takes to communicate most effectively. I'm not talking about getting physical in a disagreement. I just mean that sometimes you will need to be direct or blunt to ensure you are heard. Jesus wasn't afraid to be aggressive in his language when he knew clear communication was important (see Matthew 16:23, for example). At the end of the day, though, if your responses are in line with the Word and you have overhonored the other person, sometimes it's best to let it go.

Somewhere in the Middle

Every now and then you may find yourself caught in the middle of a conflict between fellow believers and one of the world's "sinners." Jesus found Himself in this situation a few times. On one occasion in particular He demonstrated a beautiful balance between standing firm in the truth of who He is, while treating everyone around Him with kindness and respect.

Some Pharisees caught a woman in the act of adultery. That's awkward to begin with. But then they brought the woman to Jesus to trap Him. According to the Old Testament law, a woman caught in adultery should be stoned to death (see John 8:1–6). The Pharisees knew Jesus liked to hang out with sinners, so they wanted to put Him in an impossible spot. If He told them to show her mercy, then He was breaking the law. If He told them to kill her, then He was going back on all His other teachings about grace and forgiveness.

Jesus knew the trap had been laid and refused to get dragged in. Instead, "Jesus bent down and started to write on the ground with his finger" (v. 6).

He didn't get into a debate. He didn't even engage the accusers on their terms. He just started writing in the sand. The Pharisees couldn't stand it, so they kept questioning Him, demanding an answer. Still, He didn't take the bait. He spoke to them but didn't answer their question. Instead, He answered, "Let any one of you who is without sin be the first to throw a stone at her" (v. 7).

Now, notice He didn't defend her behavior. He didn't say, "Leave her alone. She's doing what makes her happy. Who are you to judge?" No, He told them, essentially, "You're so worried about her sin that you don't even care about your own sin."

Then He stooped back down and started writing again.

Plenty have speculated as to what Jesus wrote, but, frankly, it doesn't matter. What we *can* see is how He communicated with the accusers. Some of us would have been intimidated by these guys and shied away from saying anything. I mean, they were smart and knew everything! Some of us would have lost our cool and yelled at them. Some of us wouldn't have known what to do and would have just kept quiet. But Jesus simply, clearly, and calmly addressed the accusation. He spoke the truth.

Sometimes you need to speak the truth. In those times, take a cue from Jesus and remain calm, communicate slowly and clearly, and maybe even with a quieter tone than you normally use. Certainly don't raise your voice, and definitely don't walk out on someone—even if you strongly disagree with them. If you feel like your blood is about to boil over or you're about to say something ridiculous or embarrassing, take a cue from Jesus and doodle on a napkin until you calm down. Look what happened after Jesus stooped down and wrote on the ground again: "At this, those who heard began to go away one at a time, the older ones first, until only Jesus was left, with the woman still standing there" (v. 9).

After the religious accusers finally slithered off, it was time to face the accused:

Jesus straightened up and asked her, "Woman, where are they? Has no one condemned you?"

"No one, sir," she said.

"Then neither do I condemn you," Jesus declared. "Go now and leave your life of sin." (vv. 10–11)

Again, Jesus communicated clearly and supportively to the accused. Remember, she had been publicly shamed and ridiculed—condemned! It's wise to demonstrate forgiveness and grace to the condemned, not heap more condemnation on them. Jesus asked her a simple question, affirmed that

160

condemnation would not come from Him, and challenged her to turn from the choices she had been making. It's important to remain true to God—both to the truth that adultery is sin and to the truth that God loves you, isn't mad at you, and in fact, has a better life in store that will bring you peace and joy. What you say is important! How you say it is also important, because God is a God of *relationship*.

John 3:17 says, "For God did not send his Son into the world to condemn the world, but to save the world through him." That world includes you—and your neighbor! In fact, God loves every person who ever lived and wants to be in relationship with them. He doesn't want to condemn them any more than He wants to condemn you. And in case you've forgotten, He doesn't want to condemn you! If you can remember to frame every conversation with this understanding, it will take you a long way toward connecting the truth that God loves them and isn't mad at them with the truth that they need Jesus.

Find Joy

My Sunday school teacher used to tell me every Sunday morning that I was going to hell. It brought her joy to think that's where I was going! Sometimes I think many people feel all Christians are this way, based on the way Christians have treated them. But joy is the fruit of the Spirit. It's a by-product of your fellowship with the Holy Spirit. That means there are ways you can keep joy in your life. I've already mentioned two big ones—spend time in God's Word first thing every morning and do life in community with other believers. Those two simple things will win many, many others to the Lord, because the world is an extremely lonely place for many people these days.

Here are a few other ways to keep joy in your life: when you get up in the morning, pray until you first encounter God and feel the joy of the Holy Spirit. Never tackle the problems or issues of the day without first doing that. I've been married now for twenty-eight years. If I said to Michelle, "Baby, I love you more than anyone else in the world, except for one or two other people," she wouldn't put up with that. God is the same way. I've made a lot of mistakes in my relationship with God, but spending time in His presence first thing in the morning has been like an investment that just keeps returning compound interest!

When you open your mouth to speak, always assume someone around you is hurting, and treat them, speak to them, and respond to them with compassion. You have been that hurting person many times in your own life. The Holy Spirit didn't fill up the church to have more power, but to fill up people who were hurting. It is completely unnecessary (and, in fact, I believe it's sin) to use condemnation when relating to anyone who is hurting, or anyone at all, really. Why would we heap condemnation on people who already feel condemned? Check out this warning:

> You, therefore, have no excuse, you who pass judgment on someone else, for at whatever point you judge another, you are condemning yourself, because you who pass judgment do the same things. (Rom. 2:1)

One day people will be in the presence of Jesus, and the sheep will be on His right side and the goats on His left. He'll look at the sheep and say, "I'm so proud of you; when

I was cold you gave Me something to wear. You let Me in. Good job! Let's enjoy eternity together!" And they'll respond, "We're glad we did it, but we don't remember doing that." Jesus will look at them and say, "No, it was when you were doing it for the one who was hurting—you were hooking *Me* up! I'm proud of you. Come home."

Then He'll look at the goats (I don't know the stats, but I hope we're doing well on the sheep side!) and say, "You didn't help, answer, or come to visit Me. Away from Me!" And the goats will respond, "When? We don't remember not doing that." And Jesus will look at them and say, "When you didn't do it for those around you, you were neglecting Me" (see Matt. 25:31–46).

Souls. Relationships. People are the most important thing God values. Are they important to you?

Remember that the world is hurting. I said earlier that it's a sin to heap condemnation on others. It's also unnecessary, because people already feel condemned. Nobody needs you to heap insult on their injury, even if it was their own mistake that got them where they are:

> Whoever believes in him is not condemned, but whoever does not believe stands condemned already because they have not believed in the name of God's one and only Son. (John 3:18)

Why heap condemnation on top of condemnation and weigh people down with something they already can't bear? That message contains no good news. Most of us have forgotten we have hurt a lot of people. Some people are even hurt because of us. Jesus gently reminds us that the amount of forgiveness we extend to others is in direct proportion to the amount He gives us:

> Do not judge, and you will not be judged. Do not condemn, and you will not be condemned. Forgive, and you will be forgiven. (Luke 6:37)

What? That statement does a lot to keep me in check for how I treat other people while I'm trying to live out real love. Forgiveness is always essential, and whether we choose to forgive or choose to judge and condemn, the result has lasting effects—even eternal effects if we're not careful.

Be Honest

While you're spending time with your friends and getting to know your neighbors, it's okay to be real with them about who you are and Who you know! Just don't condemn them in the process of sharing. They'll respect you for it. In fact, if you shrink back in fear or you're not sincere about your faith or you hide the truth of Who you put your trust in, you'll lose the respect of your community and neighborhood. When you hide the truth, it's really the same as lying. Of all things, honesty is one virtue people in our culture highly value across the board, regardless of their faith.

My parents had one main rule when we were kids: *don't lie*. They were always much easier on us if we owned our mistakes than if we hid them or lied about them. (Tip of the day, parents: create a safe place for your kids to be honest with you. When they own their errors, let your correction be clear but full of kindness. The kindness of God leads to repentance, and this principle works in parenting too.)

For example, Mom used to have a lamp that she loved. Well, when Mom and Dad weren't home, my brother, Randy, and I commonly played sports in the house. That wasn't our best idea one day (or any day, now that I think about it), because I threw the ball so hard that it crashed into the lamp, breaking it. I knew my mom was going to kill me, so I had to hide it. I had to cover it up.

Fortunately, it was cracked only in the back, so I positioned it perfectly, where the broken part wasn't visible from any angle. Then all I had left to do was coach my four-year-old brother on how to lie about what happened. I said, "Listen, Randy. We're not going to say anything to Mom and Dad about that lamp."

"Okay, I won't say nuthin'."

Mom and Dad pulled into the driveway, and I reminded Randy again, "Now, remember, we're not going to say anything about that lamp. You got it?"

"Okay. I'm not gonna say anything about the lamp."

As soon as our parents walked into the house, the first thing Randy said was, "While y'all was gone, Rick didn't break the lamp!" I got whipped for breaking the lamp, but I got whipped again for lying about it!

Second Corinthians 7:10 says, "Godly sorrow brings repentance that leads to salvation and leaves no regret; but worldly sorrow brings death." Worldly sorrow is when you're simply angry that you got caught. Every now and then someone gets away with a cover-up, but a cover-up is really just unconfessed sin. Have you ever seen a politician or sports figure try to cover up a scandal or personal failure? When you stop covering up, you start growing and changing into the person you want to be. The same sun that shines down on the earth will harden clay and melt wax. It just depends on what substance it's applied to.

I even believe unconfessed sin is a big reason why there's so much hatred and judgmentalism in today's culture—especially in our churches. One early sign of sin is when we critique in others what we condone in ourselves. Have you ever said about a political candidate, or any famous person, "They should be thrown under the bus for that!" When King David was confronted by Nathan for committing adultery and then covering it with murder, Nathan first told him a story of a rich man who took a poor man's only lamb and fed it to his guests. King David's initial response was, "We've got to kill that guy!" King David *was* that guy (see 2 Sam. 12).

We say the same thing—"That candidate should be in jail" or "That candidate is too stupid to run for president." Oftentimes, we're the ones who are stupid. Maybe some of us should be in jail. Sometimes judgmentalism makes us feel like we're at least better than them. But not one person is holy—no, not one. Not even you.

Conclusion

So don't be surprised if you feel caught in the middle between religious judgmentalism on one side and someone screaming that you're intolerant on the other. We live in an angry world. Please remember that the Holy Spirit is the most powerful force in the world, but He's also the gentlest. He will not knock down the walls of others' hearts to get in, so neither should you.

Or maybe as you've been reading this, the Holy Spirit has shown you how on one side you've compromised your convictions, or on the other side you've become intolerant of others. Or both! According to Acts 17:30, "These times of ignorance God overlooked, but now commands all men everywhere to repent" (NKJV). Repentance is for now. When the Holy Spirit convicts, He says, "Hey, let's settle this with God. The Father wants you around." The only way you can be prepared to repent is through conviction that comes from the Holy Spirit. He is the Spirit of comfort, the anesthesiologist before the surgery. With the Holy Spirit, failure is never final. So if that's you, now is the time to call a friend or confidant. If you see areas where you need correction, don't keep hiding them! Confess them to God and you'll be forgiven; tell a friend and you'll be healed.

9

Love Never Fails (though It Feels Like It Might)

My mom generally wasn't one to hover over us when we were growing up. She'd send us outside, tell us to go find a stick to play with, and say, "See you at dark." So we'd head outside and have a day of it. If I could find two sticks, then I'd have a *really* good time. And when we could add a rock to that—two sticks and a rock—we could play for days.

One day I had an idea that would take the stick and rock fun to a whole new level. I decided to throw rocks at every car that went by. It was awesome running away from people—until this big, black brand-new truck went by and I nailed it with a large rock. Bull's-eye! Only, when the truck pulled over after being hit, out came a man who should have been playing in the NFL. He was fast as lightning. I took three steps, and he was already right by my side. He grabbed me

169

and looked at me with such fury that I thought he was going to kill me right there. I remember thinking, *Just don't tell my mom. You can kill me, but don't tell my mom.*

"Where do you live, boy?" he screamed.

I choked under the pressure and pointed to a house nearby that I'd never been to. "I live right there, sir!" I didn't want my mom to know.

He walked straight over to the house, dragging me with him. To make matters worse, he knocked on the door. *Lord, don't let them be home*, I prayed. My prayer wasn't answered the way I wanted. A woman answered the door. She looked at this angry man she had never met, then she looked at me, who she'd also never met. "What's going on?" she asked.

"Your son's throwing rocks. You need to beat him for that!"

I was peeking around from behind him with my finger over my lips, whispering, "Shhhhh!" She was so cool about it. She said, "Oh, thank you so much. I'm so sorry. I'll take care of it." I loved that lady, right then and there. I started to relax. *Mom will never have to know.*

As soon as he left, the lady, whom I loved, turned to me and said, "Where do you live? I'm going to go tell your parents." This sweet little neighbor lady looked all protective and supportive, but no! She outed me. Let's just say I had an encounter with my mom that day that was character shaping, for sure!

It was good my mom found out what I did, because I needed some correction regarding my disrespect toward others. If I hadn't learned not to throw rocks at people back then, I might still be doing it today, though as an adult it would play out differently. I have often said that an encounter with God changes everything, and that definitely affects our relationships, how we treat other people. We can only love God and others as we have first received His love for us (1 John 4:19). That's good news right there! We go to God to receive love, and we go to people to give it.

When we receive God's love, when we have a real encounter with God, He changes us in the process. This hinges on our willingness to acknowledge Him every day, all day. The more we spend time in His presence, worshiping Him, choosing to be thankful, and honoring and obeying Him in all things, the more He changes us. The more in tune we get with the sound of His voice, the more we learn to follow His lead and the more He changes us. And the more we intercede on behalf of others in prayer, the more He changes us. And others.

Keeping It All in Context

Our society contains a growing segment of hate-filled but somehow well-meaning (and at this point I'm using this term very loosely) Christians who take every opportunity to remind others that the Bible *does say* "men who have sex with men . . . will [not] inherit the kingdom of God." (1 Cor. 6:9–10). That's an example of one of the ditches I was describing earlier that demonstrates people who live on the side of truth but offer little to no grace toward others. Let's look a little more closely at the insightful context of that verse:

> If any of you has a dispute with another, do you dare to take it before the ungodly for judgment instead of before the Lord's people? Or do you not know that the Lord's people will judge the world? And if you are to judge the world, are you not competent to judge trivial cases? Do you not know

that we will judge angels? How much more the things of this life! Therefore, if you have disputes about such matters, do you ask for a ruling from those whose way of life is scorned in the church? I say this to shame you. Is it possible that there is nobody among you wise enough to judge a dispute between believers? But instead, one brother takes another to court—and this in front of unbelievers!

The very fact that you have lawsuits among you means you have been completely defeated already. Why not rather be wronged? Why not rather be cheated? Instead, you yourselves cheat and do wrong, and you do this to your brothers and sisters. Or do you not know that wrongdoers will not inherit the kingdom of God? Do not be deceived: Neither the sexually immoral nor idolaters nor adulterers nor men who have sex with men nor thieves nor the greedy nor drunkards nor slanderers nor swindlers will inherit the kingdom of God. And that is what some of you were. But you were washed, you were sanctified, you were justified in the name of the Lord Jesus Christ and by the Spirit of our God. (1 Cor. 6:1–11)

I find it interesting that the verse that references homosexuality comes close to the end of a challenge from the apostle Paul to Christians to avoid lawsuits among one another. He posed a solution: "Why not rather be wronged? Why not rather be cheated?" He knew the Corinthians were just as guilty as everybody else, especially and more apparently in the areas of cheating and doing each other wrong. He then reminded them in verse 9, writing, "Do you not know that wrongdoers will not inherit the kingdom of God?" So, from the start, Paul lumped the behavior of the Corinthian Christians in with that of everybody else, warning them in the process not to be deceived regarding the reality of how far they had drifted. The Corinthians had become hypocrites, resolving their differences through petty lawsuits. They treated people no differently than the way everybody else did. The only "difference" was they still called themselves Christians. Sounds like a lot of Christians today, doesn't it?

I believe this passage refers to someone who has chosen cheating as a way of life or part of their identity. In verses 9–10, Paul delves further into different areas of wrongdoing, but this is not an exhaustive list. He writes, "Don't go back to doing those things, because those things have serious consequences! You know this, because some of you used to live that way." In other words, "That includes you!"

Within the context of Romans 3:23, which says, "For all have sinned and fall short of the glory of God," this passage further demonstrates that some people have a bigger struggle with certain sins than others do. For example, alcoholism is included in this list. Some of the Corinthian Christians came out of a lifestyle of alcoholism. Paul wanted them to know that because Jesus died for them, the presence of God in their lives could certainly overcome the power of alcohol in their lives. Other Corinthians came out of a lifestyle of homosexuality. Did Jesus die for them too? And can God overcome the sin of homosexuality? You know the answer is yes, but have you allowed the louder voices in our culture to overwhelm you into answering no? Have you lost courage in your convictions by allowing the world to convince you that homosexuality is not a sin? Have you lost confidence in the grace of Jesus by allowing some Christians to convince you that some people are too far gone to be redeemed? Sometimes we get hammered so frequently with the same idea that our minds and hearts feel exhausted; we shut down inside. What do you do when you feel over-whelmed and you just don't know what to do? Why not take a break?

Take a Break

Let's go back to the story in Mark 6 of the feeding of the five thousand. Remember why Jesus and the disciples crossed the lake in the first place? He started this whole mess with, "Come with me by yourselves to a quiet place and get some rest" (Mark 6:31). Let me ask you another question: Once those thousands of people showed up hungry, what did the disciples actually have to *do* to feed them? They had to find a lunch bag, tell the people to sit in groups, and then pass the food out to the heads of each group. Assuming there were twenty thousand people there that day (we don't know the exact number because five thousand was the number of adult men), each disciple would have had to pass out food to thirty-three group leaders.

Where is the "rest" in that activity? I don't know about you, but that seems like a lot of work to me, until you re-member how *many* people they were feeding. Compared to actually cooking dinner for fifteen to twenty thousand people, the disciples didn't really have to do very much at all! They must have thought to themselves, *I don't need to multiply the bread; that's God's job. I only have to be willing to be a part of the miracle.* Jesus needed only twelve people to feed a multitude.

In Psalms we find this about rest:

174

> Return to your rest, my soul,
>> for the Lord has been good to you. (Ps. 116:7)

And Jesus said,

> Come to me, all you who are weary and burdened, and I will
> give you rest. Take my yoke upon you and learn from me,
> for I am gentle and humble in heart, and you will find rest
> for your souls. (Matt. 11:28–29)

When you rest, when you honor the Lord with a Sabbath day one day a week and even a mini-Sabbath rest during the day, and when you rest just because you need to—like when you feel overwhelmed by what's going on in the culture around you—you're giving the Lord breathing room to work in your life. You're saying to God, "I don't have to strive to provide everything for my own life. Instead, in what appears to be lack in my life, I choose to believe You are my provider; You will provide for my family." You simply can't serve to your best ability, whether it's in your work, your family, or your church, if you are always tired or stressed out. Take a Sabbath day each week and a Sabbath moment each day.

And in those moments when you feel overwhelmed by what's going on in the world around you, give the battle to God and let Him fight it.

When you rest from labor, you are choosing to actively trust in God's provision for you. And when you rest, when you truly rest, your spirit rejuvenates. The Lord blesses you with new ideas and a fresh perspective. You are able to respond to others from a fresh, restful position, not from a weary one. Whether you are rested directly affects how you relate to others.

When You've Done All Else

Let's just say you've put into practice every idea I've mentioned in this book. It still doesn't guarantee you'll effectively reach the people around you with the truth that God loves them, is not mad at them, and simply wants to rescue them from themselves. And it doesn't guarantee you'll be able to communicate the truth to someone making an ungodly choice that, "Yes, if you keep standing on those tracks, you will get hit by an oncoming train, but please know I'm saying this out of *love for you*." If the estimated sixty million American believers begin communicating with one voice the truth with love and compassion, if we put our best foot forward 100 percent of the time, what else can we do? What else should we do? Pray.

Paul writes,

> I urge, then, first of all, that petitions, prayers, intercession and thanksgiving be made for all people—for kings and all those in authority, that we may live peaceful and quiet lives in all godliness and holiness. This is good, and pleases God our Savior, who wants all people to be saved and to come to a knowledge of the truth. (1 Tim. 2:1–4)

The best thing you and I can do is always to pray. Pray by yourself or with your friends or family. Pray in the morning or at night. Pray for everybody the Lord brings to mind, and don't leave out our government, for goodness' sake! In fact, verse 1 of the previous passage includes "kings and all those in authority" and clearly tells us how to pray for them—to make "petitions" (to ask, beg, press God about) and "prayers" (worshipful, earnest requests).

The next word is *intercession*, which is a complex word with a lot of meaning. The Greek word is *enteuxis*, and the root word for it, *entygchanō*, means to meet up with and have a conversation with someone to convince them of something, or for you to ultimately fall in line with them. The goal of intercession is for everyone to end up in agreement about an issue. In this context, you could say intercession is essentially taking your issue to God for as long as it takes for your position on that issue to fall in line with His will. It requires being willing to have a real conversation with Him and sincerely listening to what He has to say. Once you understand His heart and mind regarding the issue, you begin to pray His heart and mind into the world.

True intercession requires persistence, because you can't give up until you get an answer. We don't just keep having the same conversation over and over with our spouse or best friend, never expecting a response or a resolution to a problem. No, there is an answer that brings an intended result, and the result is *always* changed lives. Always.

The last word in that first verse is *thanksgiving*. How hard is it to be thankful for *all* the people around you, in your culture, and in your government? Yet the Word clearly commands us to be thankful for them. Once you've done all you know to do, continue to pray that the Lord of the harvest will have His way.

Since we are called to be Christlike, which means "like Christ," let me ask you this: How's your prayer life? Can you commit today to praying for the leaders of our nation with petitions, prayers, intercession, and thanksgiving? If you already pray regularly, can you up your game a little bit?

Maybe you could lead a prayer group once a week. Or go early to work and pray over your workplace before the day starts. Start praying for people who are normally outside your circle of influence. If you're already doing that, keep it up! Persevere and persist until you get an answer, more specifically when you see the Lord having His way. The Lord wants to hear from you, and as you are one of His representatives here on the earth, He loves it when you partner with Him in your prayer life to effect change in the world. It's the way He designed this place.

Sometimes when you're in the middle of praying for a solution, it's quite possible you may begin to understand God is also calling you to take a step toward being part of the answer! A pastor once had a dream of two homeless women praying for food. Suddenly, a loaf of bread fell from heaven, and one of the ladies caught it. In the dream, the pastor turned to God and asked, "Why did you answer one woman's prayers and not the other's?" God told him, "I did! I answered both. I meant for her to give half of that to the other lady, but she kept it all to herself." This pastor began to see that God often answers our prayers by giving us the opportunity to be an active part of the solution.

Stand

My primary hope is to take the church back to Jesus so that we represent His character and nature more fully and accurately in a culture that is increasingly losing its compass. And when you know you've done all you know to do—you've loved the best you know how and you've prayed your heart out—stand firm. Stand in truth and stand in love. Don't compromise your convictions, no matter what those around you are doing. Check out this familiar but encouraging passage from Ephesians 6:18–20:

> And pray in the Spirit on all occasions with all kinds of prayers and requests. With this in mind, be alert and always keep on praying for all the Lord's people. Pray also for me, that whenever I speak, words may be given me so that I will fearlessly make known the mystery of the gospel, for which I am an ambassador in chains. Pray that I may declare it fearlessly, as I should.

Paul wouldn't have asked to be fearless in sharing the gospel if he wasn't in intimidating circumstances. He wrote the book of Ephesians while under house arrest in Rome under Emperor Nero, by far the most ruthless leader of the Roman Empire. Nero murdered his wife, his stepbrother, and even his own mother. Who does that? A crazed lunatic. Nero's fierce, inhumane cruelty toward Christians is well-documented, as he commonly had them burned alive, crucified, or fed to wild animals.

So Paul had every reason to feel afraid or intimidated, as it was quite clear what the consequence would be if he followed through with speaking the truth of God's love for the Romans. But Paul was also a man of faith. I love the way he conquered fear. His accusers said, "We're gonna throw you in prison!" and he replied, "Good! I have some letters I need to write." They said, "We're gonna kill you!" and he replied, "Good! I'll be with the Lord!"

Psalm 34:4 says, "I prayed to the LORD, and he answered me. He freed me from *all* my fears" (NLT, emphasis added). All of them! When you go through the Word of God and see the heroes of the faith, those who made a difference, many of them were extremely afraid, even of the culture around them. When God challenged Jonah to do something, Jonah was so afraid that he ran in the exact opposite direction of where God wanted him to be (see Jon. 1:3). And God called Gideon a mighty warrior when he was hiding in the ground, totally afraid of the enemy he knew he needed to face (see Judg. 6:11–12).

Fear cannot exist when you see God as a loving Father. The Word of God essentially says in many places, "Do not be afraid; your Father will take care of you!" If you will go with the presence of God, with His Spirit living inside of you, He will give you peace, He will carry you, and He will give you joy. Remember that "the LORD will rescue his servants; no one who takes refuge in him will be condemned" (Ps. 34:22).

Chick-fil-A recently demonstrated in an incredible way how to love your neighbor while remaining true to your convictions. On June 12, 2016, a gunman opened fire at a gay nightclub in Orlando, murdering forty-nine people and injuring dozens more. As word of the shooting spread, employees of local Chick-fil-A restaurants in Orlando showed up that morning to cook and donate food for law enforcement and blood donors. The remarkable thing is they did all this on a Sunday. A restaurant that has been closed on Sundays since 1946 chose to open its doors that day. Why? "We love this city and love the people in our community," Chick-fil-A announced.* The company didn't shrink back in fear, and they didn't use the fact that it was their Sabbath day as an excuse not to get involved or show they cared.

*Todd Starnes, "Chick-fil-A Did WHAT on Sunday?" Fox News, June 14, 2016, http://www.foxnews.com/opinion/2016/06/14/chick-fil-did-what-on-sunday .html.

Conclusion

Immediately after He fed the five thousand, Jesus retreated to the hills. *As usual*. The disciples went to wait for Him at the shore of the Sea of Galilee. *As usual!* (see Matt. 14:22–23). When He hadn't returned by nightfall, they chose to go ahead without Him and started rowing across the sea. The Sea of Galilee is around eight miles wide, so the disciples were committing to a long, hard row. By themselves. In the dark. It had already been a very long day, so I'm sure they were physically spent before they even started.

Well, a storm came through when they were in the center of the lake, so they were really in a do-or-die moment. When it felt like things couldn't get any worse, Jesus showed up, walking on the water.

The frightened disciples didn't know what to do, but Jesus calmly engaged them: "It is I; don't be afraid" (John 6:20). They let Him in the boat, and in my opinion, a fascinating miracle occurred at that moment. The Bible says, "Immediately the boat reached the shore where they were heading" (v. 21). What? That's amazing! Who needs a teleporter when you've got Jesus?

At times, we may feel like everything is building up to the perfect storm around us. I am writing this during what is surely the wildest political season our country has experienced to date, and I have no idea if our world will get even darker or if we've already hit gale-force winds. It sure seems like we have. Maybe you even feel like you're in a boat by yourself with no real hope for rescue. Take heart, and don't be afraid. Have courage, because I do know one thing: Jesus will show up. And when He does, you will immediately arrive at your destination.

When we get to heaven someday and fully see the awesomeness, power, and majesty of God, there's a chance we'll look back on our lives and think, *Why didn't we do more? Why were we so afraid? Why did we hesitate every day?* The way you relate to your world can cause the people around you to encounter real love in an angry world. Don't be afraid. Take the next step. Do it today.

Acknowledgments

I am thankful for my family for being in ministry with me each and every day for the last twenty-nine years: my wife, Michelle; my four children—Hunter, Hailee, Tanner, and Grace; and now my son-in-law, Luke; my daughter-in-law, Katy; and our new grandson, Jack. I could not have written this book without your faithfulness and patience through the years—each one of you! Thank you for the way you love God, love life, and love our ministry together.

Rick Bezet is the founder and lead pastor of New Life Church in Central Arkansas, listed by *Outreach Magazine* in 2009 as America's fastest-growing church. Today, with more than a dozen campuses and a multitude of worship experiences, New Life Church has a rapidly expanding vision of reaching the state of Arkansas with the message of God's love. Author of *Be Real*, Rick is one of the founding directors of the Association of Related Churches (ARC), an organization designed to impact the world through missions. He lives in Arkansas with his wife, Michelle, and their four children.

NEW LIFE CHURCH

NEW LIFE CHURCH EXISTS TO
CONNECT PEOPLE TO THE
LOVE OF GOD, THE HOPE
OF JESUS, AND THE FAMILY
WITHIN HIS CHURCH.

JOIN OUR WEEKEND SERVICES ONLINE AT
LIVE.NEWLIFECHURCH.TV

TWITTER.COM/NEWLIFECHURCHTV
FACEBOOK.COM/NEWLIFECHURCH
INSTAGRAM.COM/NEWLIFECHURCHTV

The Association of Related Churches is an organization that provides financial support, resources, and relationships you can count on at every turn. For more information on launching a church with the ARC, visit **ARCCHURCHES.COM.**

Check out ARCCHURCHES.COM/JOIN for more details on becoming a part of our mission as a partner or member.

Together, we are making a difference!

ARCCHURCHES.COM